The

Golden

of a

Irish Emigrant

Step By Step

By

Simon Corkery

ARTHUR H. STOCKWELL LTD.
Elms Court Ilfracombe
Devon

First published in Great Britain, 1991

ISBN 0 7223 2532-0

Printed in Great Britain by
Arthur H. Stockwell Ltd.
Elms Court Ilfracombe
Devon

Dedication

To my father and mother, to Fr. John and all my brothers and sisters in Longford. To my six children — John, Angela, Eileen, Elizabeth, Simon and Sarah. To my sixteen grand children.

To my darling wife Elsie for the help in compiling and researching this book.

FOREWORD

I have known Simon and Elsie Corkery for many years and I have always been impressed with their unfailing good humour. It was only when they showed me the manuscript of this book that I realised how much more there was to know about this couple now in the Autumn of their lives.

As a young man Simon left our shores, as did so many of his generation, to seek a new life in England. The tale he has to tell of his progress through life, with its many journeys and adventures is in many ways quite extraordinary. He has a wonderful memory for recalling people, places and incidents and the stories are told with great kindness and good humour.

It seems to me that the book is in the great tradition of Irish story telling. Here we have an emigrant who spent most of his life away from his native country. Now back in his beloved Ireland he has taken the time and trouble to record the details of what was a most eventful and at times exciting life.

I am certain that those who know Simon and Elsie will read the book with great interest. But it will also provide hours of enjoyable reading for members of the general public, lucky enough to obtain a copy.

Good Luck with your literary endeavours Simon, and may the Lord spare the health of your wife, family and yourself.

Jim O'Keeffe.

Myself and my wife Elsie

CHAPTER I

I was born in Ardagh Village in Co. Longford on the 11th of April in the year 1919, my Father was a Corkman, and my Mother was from Longford. Daddy taught in Loughill National School, and our house, which rang with laughter of three happy children was a neat little dwelling house. Then the day of sorrow approached, my Mother died shortly after giving birth to Patrick Joe, who also passed away.

It was out of this sad parting of my dear mother that life really began, with strange unknown feelings of a future that was to be filled with happy memories and also with sad ones. My Aunt Maud took upon herself the responsibility of taking John the eldest boy, Lily May the youngest, and of course, myself, second in command, from our home in Longford to Ballygurteen in County Cork, where my Granny and Aunt Madge stood in the doorway and beside them a huge Irish Terrier named Harry, who did not approve at first but later was to be our devoted companion for walks. We settled in as children usually do, to our new surroundings, with Granny laying before us the habits of life, that were to be the moulding of our whole lives in the days ahead. She was a strong, tall woman of certain dignity, whose hair was rolled in a top knot on her head, giving her a sort of crown that the Grannies of today can never treasure. Aunt Madge, was of course, the mainstay of all that Granny desired; she cooked, washed, and saw to all our requirements in a kind and firm manner. It was she who taught us our prayers and started us with lessons, and so the great day arrived when I was to go to school.

John had already started and it was Mary Kate O'Connell who took me to school the first day, and then I was to meet Miss McSweeney, the head mistress and Miss Murray the junior or infant teacher. My arrival at Ballygurteen National School was one of fear as well as interest, in that I met Peter Kingston there, and a few other boys. But there was only one thing we were not allowed to do, and that was to play with the other children in the school playground. If our clothes were dirty when we came home, we got a hiding from Aunty for it. So we galloped to school in the morning, returned to dinner at mid-day, and ran back again to continue to learn and play in plasticine. At this stage it is only right to mention that Aunt Maud who had brought us from Longford, had returned to England to take up her position, which she gave up to nurse my mother during her illness.

The next thing of importance was the day I took Lily May by the hand to school. Everyone in the village knew, because I shouted the glad tidings to everyone that morning. Tim Carthy now dead, 'Lord have mercy on him' was our landlord, of course he had to know, so did the Sullivans and Mr. and Mrs George Kingston. Our Parish Priest Fr. Daly, 'Lord rest his soul', came to school and seemed to take a great interest in us. I used to borrow his ebony walking stick and ride it for a horse, he was always amazed at how our little legs used to bear up under us as we walked up the hills to Mass at Rossmore Church on Sunday mornings with Aunt Madge.

Saturday night was a great night for preparation for Sunday, boots polished, hair washed, ironing and everything was completed by Aunt Madge so that, we were looked up to and admired as being well cared for as we went into the front seat in the Western aisle in Rossmore Church. There we listened Sunday after Sunday to Fr. Daly preaching his long sermons. In one of these sermons I will always remember the way he pointed to the door of the Western aisle and as Tim Sullivan went out, feeling sickly, I could hear Fr. Daly say in a clear distinct voice, 'and that man is now on his way to Perdition which was one of his great phrases, used to describe the damnation of a man's immortal soul.'

The years passed, John received his First Holy Communion and he looked very smart in his white suit. So it was also, that when my First Holy Communion came along I was dressed in a similar suit and Lily May in her little white frock and veil made it a day that will always be remembered by us. Not only was it a happy one for my Aunt Madge, but also for us, because it was one of those days when little luxuries like sweet cake for tea and sweets were really appreciated and also the hosts of friends that shared with us that spiritual joy on these great occasions.

Ballygurteen then will always be treasured as a place dear to my heart, the friendly neighbours, like the Kingstons, the McCarthys, the Hurley family who supplied us with milk, the Harringtons, whose joys we shared with Bessie and Madge. Mr. Stanley who supplied our foodstuffs, who never forgot us at Christmas time. Uncle Nelius from Cork who always sent his Xmas box, and who we saw for those two days each year, Christmas Day and St. Stephen's Day.

Then every summer Uncle Michael would come on holidays from Scotland, where he was teaching and take us out in the side car of his motor cycle. These trips I really enjoyed because it made a change from going to the well for water with a sweet gallon, and the boredom of lessons all the time. But don't think that Daddy had forgotten us during those years! He came when he could, I remember on one occasion I was so overjoyed I could not wait to get a drink of water to quench my thirst, when I was going to meet him. I stooped over the river bank of the nearest river, and fell in, soaking the lovely suit of clothes Aunt Madge had ironed so nicely for me that morning. He brought with him on this occasion, a bicycle for John, and that bicycle was handed down to me and afterwards to Lily May.

The years passed quickly until John was confirmed, which was another great occasion and John was so small and young that his Lordship the Bishop questioned Monsignor Hill about him, but Catechism was his best subject, and he was brighter than boys of twice his age. In the meantime in Longford, Daddy had already married again, this time to a former pupil of his. To us it made little difference, we had got used to living with Aunt Madge and Granny that we passed it off as something that normally happens in the course of time, at least for me, Longford was just a place on the map of Ireland, and no more. John, of course, went to live in Longford and went to Daddy's school, thereby breaking up as it were, the threefold childish happiness which had existed between us.

Miss McSweeney who always took a delight in making me kneel down in a corner of the room for being naughty, retired, and young Master McCarthy took over, although I was rather lonely losing Miss McSweeney, I was glad to have a male teacher, because the boys needed some encouragement in games etc.

It was not long after this that Lily May and I were confirmed, and I had a light grey suit for my examination day and a velvet suit for my day of Confirmation. Aunt Maud had brought everything with her from London and she made Lily May look really smart. Bishop Roche, who examined me asked me who washed my face that morning, as he could see himself in the shine that was on my face, and I told him, "My Aunty, My Lord" had washed it, and he asked me what kind of soap did she use, "Ordinary soap my Lord" said I, which made him really laugh. The happy years Lily May and I had spent after this soon drew to a close, when I was told I would have to return to Daddy's new home in Longford. I will never forget how it broke my heart to leave my friends in Ballygurteen. Aunt Madge was broken hearted, and so was Granny. Granny was full of advice as usual, and Uncle Michael travelled to Longford with me. This was a sad day for Lily May and for me, there were new interests, new source of life, and a stepmother to get used to.

Fr John, Lily May and myself.

My Confirmation in Rossmore, left to right: Aunt Maud, Fr O'Dwyer, Bishop Roche, Aunt Madge. Front: Lily May and self.

CHAPTER II

I travelled with Uncle Michael from 7.30 a.m. until 10.00 p.m. when I arrived at Longford Station, I was met by Daddy, after which we travelled by car to a country thatched house, where I was made welcome by my stepmother, whom I always referred to as Baby. She was friendly and homely, and so were her father and mother, (Mr. & Mrs. John Farrell). And then, of course, I met the young family, who were dashing about in their night clothes. There was Mary Teresa, Michael and Kathleen, and it was with this great family that I had to spend my future years. John, of course, by this time had succeeded in gaining a scholarship to St. Mels College, Longford, where he was a boarder. Everything seemed so strange, my heart ached for Ballygurteen, and the life I had been so used to, but with Baby's father around me constantly taking an interest in me, I soon forgot my sorrows, and settled down to life on the farm, and trips to the bog with him. They tried me out as a jockey on their donkey and when I was firmly established, as I thought, on the donkey's back, John who was on holiday from College stuck a nail in the donkey's behind, and I was left lying in a grassy field and the donkey was running by himself, to the laughter of all, especially Baby's father.

Then to my father's school, which I had seen as a baby, I returned to be enrolled as his pupil in preparation for my entrance to a secondary college. I liked to be taught by Daddy, and I made friends quickly in Longford. We all used to go to Mass in the old jaunting car. Baby herself, was the first person to show me my mothers grave at the back of Ardagh Church where I had been baptised. The thing I enjoyed most about Longford was the visit by night of the old farmers, who sat around the fireside spinning tales of what happened long ago, and telling ghost stories, that would make you afraid to go outside in the dark in case you met some of the creatures they yarned about. I made good friends with Neddy Rogers and Jimmy Halligan and John Joe Farrell. It was from John Joe's mother that I learned quite a lot about what a good person my mother was and what a great dancer she was. Derrymore was the district where we lived, and I forgot Ballygurteen for the time being, because my mind was fully occupied about the fishing I used to do, although not very successfully. I was always at the books, even after school hours, because Daddy was teaching Jimmy Halligan and myself for the entrance examination to St. Mel's College. I liked the Haymaking season and the cutting of the corn, it was a time of laughter where I was concerned and Baby's mother was such an expert cook, I loved to eat her pancakes for tea. It was she who always took my part, and we formed a great riendship which lasted for many years later. The children were growing up to be fine sturdy children and they loved to play with me, even indoors, much to the displeasure of Daddy, because he could not hear the news on the wireless set. Anyhow, the time came for my examination to leave the Primary School, this I passed with flying colours, but not so with my entrance examination to St. Mel's College. Jimmy Halligan passed, but I didn't, much to Daddy's

Granny Farrell

St. Mel's College

Daddy in later years

disappointment. I now found myself the black sheep of the family, people advising me, even the neighbours were always pointing out to me what a great scholar my brother John was. It was true, but the more I saw the books, the more boring it became. I wanted so much to play with the other boys, but Daddy was very strict, I remember on one occasion, when I was attending his school, our class got a test paper to do, and we were told if we were finished early, we could go home early. Anyhow, Daddy went to see Miss Shannon, the school mistress, and when his back was turned I went to his drawer and took out the answer book. I then made up some formula and put the answers underneath. Of course Daddy returned meantime and asked if any body had finished their test cards. Up went my hand, and he asked me to bring over my work to him to examine it. Of course, he knew I was telling lies and I was told to leave the school. This I did, and with the humiliation of going home, and everybody asking me along the road, what had happened, I made up my mind I should not go through that again. But that was not the last of my trouble, there was an old lady at the corner of the road, and she used to get water for her donkey from the river by reaching her bucket down at the deepest part of the river which was under the bridge where there was a stepping stone. This evening Neddy Rogers and Johnny and myself dammed the river with stones and grass sods, making it possible to catch trout in the shallow water. This old lady came out and put her bucket down for water, but could get none. We could see her under the bridge so we left the dam go and she got a bucket of dirty water. It was then that the swearing started, she was going for the Master, meaning my Daddy, as he was always known as that in the neighbourhood. We even threw a stone into her bucket, sending it flying out of her hands. This sort of devilment appealed to me whenever I got away with it, but Daddy noticed that I was carrying my socks and boots in my hands, so the truth was out again. It is memories such as these, that make life worth living.

Then one sad evening brought sorrow to all Derrymore. Johnny Farrell 'Lord have mercy on him', went to the races at Arva on the borders of Longford and Cavan, and he asked me to meet him with the donkey and cart in town that night. He went to the races with a neighbour, Joe Donovan and after a pleasant day, there he was on the bus ready to come home, when he dropped dead, and I was told as I got into town. It was a great blow for me because we had had great times together, and I felt his loss very much indeed, as he had always been so good to me, his wife and Baby were distracted. The farm passed on to Daddy, and a new house was built.

In the meantime Daddy had sent me to the Presentation College in Cork, but after one year I came home again. Before I came home I paid a visit to Ballygurteen, where there were a few changes. Lily May had grown older now, but Aunt Madge had not changed much, she was pleased to see me. Uncle Michael gave up teaching shortly after this in Killoe Parish where he had been for some years. He used to come to Longford from time to time to see us. He succeeded in getting a big school in Rossmore in Cork and bought a huge farm of land with it. So it was that Lily May, Aunt Madge and Granny went to live in Rossmore with him.

When I returned home after my stay at the Presentation College, it was to a disappointed father. He then sent me to the Christian Brothers school in Baldoyle in Dublin; where I thought I had found a vocation at last. I was very lonely at first, but I soon settled in, and although the Religious life was hard, I seemed to be at peace there and I settled more to my studies there than before. On the football field too, I picked up, and I really enjoyed our walks to Howth and the sea at Portmarnock was magnificent for swimming. But again, it seems those in authority thought I was not steady enough, and so back to Longford I went more disappointed than ever. Daddy was now at his wits end to know what to do with me, but if there is no vocation there you cannot force it, so at last I was sent to St. Mel's College to follow in the footsteps of John who had gained another place into Maynooth College to continue his studies for the priesthood.

My three years at St. Mel's were pleasant ones, but again although I thought I was studying as hard as anybody else, my efforts on examination day were not satisfactory, I again made many friends among my school pals and I became football crazy, and every minute I had to myself I was out on the field. I got punished, I was wild and without balast, such were the reports that came home to Daddy, who by this time, was disgusted beyond words. So it was decided that I should stay at home and work on the farm.

This was the real breaking down; neighbours asked me why I did not succeed like John after all the money my father had spent on me? It is hard to hear it from your own family, but when the neighbours question you to know why you did not succeed, it becomes unbearable. Throughout all this disappointment, Baby's mother remained my staunch friend, and anytime anybody said anything she would say "Simon will show them all yet". Well, I tried every trick in the book to get jobs either at home or in England, but Daddy always got my letters first. I worked in the bog, helping Jim Donlan, a neighbour and great friend, and I even helped him to build the house in which he now lives. It took my mind off of other things, and we had some great times together. I read Sexton Blake novels, I lived in my dreams in Hay Market Street and Soho and other parts of London, until I knew London mentally as it were, from Charing Cross Road to Victoria Station.

Then Eddy McCord a pupil of Daddy's came home on holiday, and he encouraged Daddy to send me to England. Gradually, after much persuasion, I got his consent to apply for a position as a Male Nurse in a hospital in London. I had the application form signed and sent back and so the date was set for me to travel to London where Eddie McCord and John Joe Donlan would meet me on my arrival. So it was with a sad heart that once again in my young life I was torn apart from the place I had grown to love and people who had known my mother. I was going further afield than any one of our family had ever done before. I said goodbye to all the Donlan family, to Neddy Rogers, Johnny and Tommy and to the Halligans, to the O'Farrells and to Canon McCabe, who has

Colaiste Iosep Naoṁṫa, Baile Dubġaill

Co. Baile Áṫa Cliaṫ

Coláiste Ullmucain na mBráṫar

St.. Joseph's College, Baldoyle, Co. Dublin

Juniorate of the Irish Christian Brothers

since passed away 'Lord have mercy on him. Baby took me to town to get me a new suit and shirts and warm underwear and as the time approached for leaving, my feelings were mixed, some were feelings of enterprise and others with a fear that after all this time I could not succeed and once again be a disappointment and heartbreak to my father. It was a sad parting, especially from Daddy and Baby's mother; and of course, the children of the family who had increased in number over the years. There was Mary Teresa, Michael, Kathleen, Celene, Philomena and not forgetting the baby of the family Angela, who I had grown to love as if she were my own child.

My father and Baby

CHAPTER III

Baby and I went to Longford Station together, and I could not resist the tears when she poured forth advice into my ear; such endearing phrases, "Mind your religion a Mac (my son), Don't forget to write often, look after your money, and God bless you". It could not have been said better had my own mother been there. Then I suddenly realised I was to be on my own from there out, and out of the corner of my eye, I noticed a nice girl carrying a bag, and the label on it told me she was going to England. Baby introduced her to me, and asked her to look after me on the way over. So it was in the company of Chrissie Skelly from Ballymahon that I travelled away from Longford Station. My tears were flowing fast at this time, but with Chrissie beside me to talk to it seemed easier.

So it was that I crossed the Irish sea in the evening of August 1938. We talked of home and of the different things that had been foremost in our lives. Above all, I was interested to learn that Chrissie had already been nursing in England, and she was able to give me a preview of what was in store for me. I slept on the boat feeling sickly at times, but thanks to Chrissie's advice, I did not feel too bad, then towards 1 a.m. I saw the shores of England, my new home as it were, stretching out its arms to welcome me, and so to Holyhead, and at last we were on the train bound for London, but of course, Chrissie got off at Rugby. I was lonely once again, it was breaking the last link of home, but soon I settled down and looked forward to meeting Eddie and John Joe at Euston.

We arrived at Euston at 7 a.m. and there sure enough were Eddie and John Joe, and Johnny McLoughlin, who had come to meet his two sisters, who had travelled over as well, and whom I did not recognise until I was introduced to them. Then I went for some breakfast and greedily devoured bacon and eggs, when about an hour afterwards I realised I had eaten bacon on Friday, and felt I had already let down my Irish heritage.

After a few hours sleep, Eddie took me to Camberwell House, South East London, where he introduced me to Sister Haddock, who made me welcome. The Hospital at first gave me a rather dreaded feeling because it had chains looping from pillar to pillar, and it had a grey drab look about it, that almost seemed to say, out of here you will never again see daylight. Eddie took his departure, and promised to see me as soon as he could. How grateful I was to have such a friend as staunch as he was.

After meeting the other male nurses and sisters, I wrote home to Daddy to say I had arrived and everything had gone according to plan, but my heart was breaking with loneliness. Gone were the green fields I had grown to love, no fresh smell of turf cutting, no longer could I hear the song of birds, but I realised that all that was behind me now. I had to face a harsh world with no pity for greenhorn just over from the Emerald Isle. Instead, I was to earn my living, and I dreaded the next morning starting at 7.30 a.m. with a white coat and

1938 — at the start of my nursing career at Camberwell House, South East London.

a bundle of keys and a whistle. How strange it all seemed; yesterday I was full of adventure, and today shy and retiring.

I was put to the test to prove my worth in caring for the mentally ill. I stood for a few moments in that dining hall surrounded by patients before I got my white coat, and I was left on my own. A patient approached me and asked me for a match, but directly I was on my guard, and was pleased when Sister McDonnell who came from Co. Roscommon, gave me my white coat and keys with a whistle attached. It was with relief I saw this patient retire to his seat watching me cautiously. I was now allotted to the Male Infirmary Ward, which was run by Sister McDonnell, it was with her guidance, that I made headway in my own nursing career, and I enjoyed every minute of it, although the hours were long and the work was heavy at times. There were some really depressing cases, it was really pathetic to see men from professions in life, living in a world apart from all the rest. There were some nice lads among the male nurses, but some of them had got smart, or at least they tried to impress me with the way they could drink, and I had the unfortunate experience of going for a grapefruit with one of them one night and finding that my grapefruit was having a double whiskey put in it, much to his surprise I walked home, but had I a headache! It was only later I discovered why. From then on I was on my guard. I chose Henry Duffy as my constant companion, and of course, I found my way to Eddie's place on several occasions. He was delighted I had settled in, and Daddy was also. I sent home money when I could afford it, and after a while I started going out with the female nurses for walks. I was rather shy, and as I had not accomplished the dash of other young fellows, they were not greatly impressed and I was just as happy at a picture on my own than if I was at a dance. But then one evening, I stayed on to listen to a patients private tale of woe, and it came to the notice of the sister. When Christmas came, she made me go dancing with a crowd of Irish nurses. Henry Duffy took me along with him. So I embarked on a new phase of life I had not tried before, as I was never allowed go dancing back home.

At first my dancing was very poor, and I found it difficult to get a partner, and time and time again the girls would walk off and leave me standing there humiliated and hurt. I found it rather tiring after working from 7.15 a.m. to 8.15 p.m. and so I always left early. We had an Irish Club in Peckham, and soon I began to make friends, but I never had the courage to take a girl home, or even to ask her. But I also had the lectures to attend to after duty hours so that my off duty soon went quickly.

I got in touch with Aunt Maud, who as you remember had taken such an interest in us after my mother's death, and who was now a dispenser in a hospital in Chatham. It was a wonderful reunion for both of us as I had not seen her for a few years, as ever she was anxious that I should be smartly dressed, and thereafter started a friendship that has lasted between us over the years. She was a great guidance to me, but she always deplored how foolishly I spent my money. She made enquiries to know if I had kept up with my religion, and thanks be to God I was pleased to say that after twelve months in England I was

H.M.S Mauretania

Eric Neilson and friends — H.M.S. Mauretania

still faithful to Mass and the Sacraments, and the Rosary, which was a thing I always treasured from the days I spent in Derrymore.

English people were honest and treated you with respect as long as you did not enter into any religious or political arguments. Meantime, world affairs and news bulletins on the B.B.C. became more alarming, and everywhere there were signs on everyones face that sooner or later, World War would come about, although the average man on the street thought some way or other that Hitler might respect the promise he made to Mr. Chamberlain at Munich.

It was also at this time that the Irish Republican Army had started throwing bombs in London, and every Irish man and woman from then on were treated with suspicion, and it made it very difficult for the Irish already in London. I was lucky our Medical Superintendent was marvellous and trusted his staff implicitly, which was ninety per cent Irish. Others were not so lucky, and lost their positions and had to return to their native soil.

My interest was in my patients and I had no desire to be drawn into politics, so I settled down to the country of my adoption with interest. Then the fateful day arrived. England declared war on Germany on the third of September 1939, and in the same breath the siren went off and so started the chaos in the Male Infirmary that afternoon. We were tidying up everywhere and no sooner had the Prime Minister finished speaking than the siren went off and everyone lost control of themselves, until Sister Haddock appeared and told us all to take the patients quickly to the ground floor, where there were easy chairs. It was with skill she organised everything and you could see that the training of the 1914-18 War was still foremost in her training. After this, we lived from one Air Raid Siren to the next, but we adapted ourselves to it as part of our daily lives. All the nurses were taught fire drill, and we had to train ourselves to act promptly and efficiently.

The male nurses nearly all joined the forces. It was difficult for boys from Ireland to join as we had to prove beyond doubt that we had no connection with the Irish Republican Army.

The days passed, London's Hyde Park was no longer a place for courting couples, air raid shelters appeared everywhere. Every part of England was mobilised, everyday dress was discarded, various coloured uniforms appeared instead. Anti aircraft guns appeared everywhere. London by night was a dark city, as if it were a city of mourning. No more could you see the little coffee stall at the corner when you came home from a dance late. Night life in that city, once a gay city, seemed to disappear, but the Cockney still kept his humour. It was during the war indeed that the people became warm hearted and friendly, people had to share each other's fate, not knowing who was next to be buried beneath the debris.

I moved from Camberwell House to the Royal Hospital for Incurables in Putney, these patients needed nursing, but there was a feeling of contentment here that was lacking at Camberwell. The pay was better, and the hours were shorter. It was also a more conservative part of London, and the surrounding district was more picturesque. I spent a happy time here, as Stephen Kelly who was at Camberwell was also with me.

Before I moved to Putney, I had the pleasure of celebrating my 21st Birthday, by taking out a charming girl named Agnes O'Leary from West Cork. We went to see John McCormack at the Queens Hall in London as he was giving a concert for the troops. It was an all star cast, the world's famous pianist Paderewski, the world's famous violinist Julie Durangi, and of course, none other could be greater in my eyes than Count John McCormack. The following evening she got me to go to see Lupino Lane in 'Me and My Girl' at the Victoria Palace. I suddenly found myself emerging into manhood as it were, and how seriously I started taking life was well demonstrated when I had an appointment with Agnes a few nights after, to my disappointment she never turned up, and I waited at the appointed spot for some hours hoping and trusting that she would turn up. Then I received some advice from an old friend who told me that I would have many disappointments with the opposite sex before I would meet the right one. I met Agnes some time later at a dance and she apologised but I had taken her so seriously that she thought it best not to see me under the circumstances, and it seems that someone else had her on his promised list. Still, to me that was a bitter disappointment because it was from her I learned to waltz, my favourite dance to this day. After that, I started to take the nicest one I saw on the dance floor and I became more cautious than before, as to how serious I should become.

I made many friends indeed and so it was that one day on my day off I went to the Air Ministry, and having seen tne photos of Pilots on the window, all I wanted to do was join the Royal Air Force, so I made some enquiries. It took some time before I finally was sent for, and after a wedding party of one of the nurses at the hospital to a fellow who had just returned from Dunkirk, that I found myself at Croydon for a medical examination.

I was passed O.K. and so on to Uxbridge for a thorough medical examination and educational examination for aircrew and I was passed fit, but I could not pass the fitness test for fighter pilot, but I was put on the list as a wireless operator, air gunner. This was a great achievement, but things were not so nice. That night we were marched to the dining hall where we were given a spoon and a fork to eat our first service meal, and later we were all sent to our sleeping quarters, but there was no mattress on the bed so I slept on my overcoat which I put over the springs of the bed. The next day I had a lovely impression of wire springs on my left thigh, and of course it was a great laugh to hear the other chaps moaning about their entry into the R.A.F. At two o'clock that afternoon we took the oath of allegiance to the King, and we were fully pledged members of the R.A.F.

I got back to the hospital to receive messages of congratulations and to receive two extra weeks pay. So I said my good-byes to civilian clothes, and after a holiday at my Aunt's, I reported to Blackpool for my six weeks training

Jack Doyle

Happy days in Blackpool

CHAPTER IV

December 6th 1940 was my entry day into Royal Air Force in Blackpool where I was fitted out with uniform, kit bag etc. my dream had come true, I felt I had achieved something worthwhile at last, and with stout heart, I shivered in my P.T. shorts in the South shore of Blackpool promenade. The days passed quickly, and after passing out as a fully fledged airman, we were posted to St. Evel Airfield in Cornwall.

This was so different from Blackpool, that we were bitterly disappointed, because after duty hours in Blackpool, we had a great choice of dance halls to go to, and another thing, we were in civilian billets. We were posted there as ground defence crew to cover the airfield from German aircraft, and we were soon mobilised into training, we soon got used to using machine guns, and to bayonet charging. When we had successfully finished the course, we felt more equipped to deal with any German than we had done before, and we were soon divided up on the different gunposts. But the great doubt remained in our minds that we would never get posted on our aircrew training, which we were originally promised, and we were told that we could put the badge of G.G. Ground Gunners on our tunics. It was satisfying to see our Blenheims taking off every night, and also our bombers to attack and bomb Germany, and also we had the sad spectacle of seeing only a few of these aircraft return. We even had German aircraft follow ours on their return flight, and try to land on one of our runaways after our landing lights had been put up for our aircraft. I was always glad to see daybreak, as it was at night that the enemy seemed to drop his bombs.

I felt really thrilled one night when we were told that there was an enemy aircraft overhead, and to shoot should he come in the target zone. I was bareheaded as I listened to Squadron Leader Gould dishing out his orders on the telephone, I had my finger on the air vickers gun at the ready for immediate action. But no such luck came my way, it fell to the fighter aircraft, the two Whirl-winds to chase him out to sea. A few days later it was reported that a Dornier had had been shot down and the pilots washed ashore. The nights were often cold, and I remember one night particularly as I thought up a poem in my mind and next morning I put it down in writing, calling it
'B Gunpost Soliloquy':

Beside a vickers gun I stood
Dressed in a coat of clay, and an iron hood
The moon shone bright
As the cliffs of Cornwall came in sight.
Defence control rang through once more
To say the Hun was once again approaching our shore
I gazed and gazed but all in vain
The only Hun I saw was the gun post rat
Who seemed to like the rain
One by one those rats did gnaw

Until at last, it sounded like (the voice of)
Lord Haw Haw
I thought of my loved ones far away
And wished that my seven days leave were on their way
I stood there lonely and depressed
Like a ship shipwrecked and distressed
But the day will come when life will be gay
And on B Gunpost I shall not have to stay.

Thoughts such as these were foremost in every airmans heart, some thought of the day when they would return to a better world where peace would reign in men's hearts.

One morning the airmen in our shift for gunpost duty were detailed to train hard for the arrival of the Duke of Kent, as we were to be the guard of honour. Everyone seemed to do their drill perfectly except myself and Sgt. McIntosh V.C. told me to hold my rifle properly and not to sling it round my neck like a clothes line. When we went back to the hut everyone started making a laugh of me. So I did nothing more than go down to the sick bay and borrow a large pad of cotton wool, and put it inside the shoulders of my RAF tunic so that my shoulders were able to make the rifle lie close to the shoulders without sliding off, as I had rather round shoulders. As we left the hut to go on parade I told some of the bright airmen that the Duke of Kent would recognise a smart airman when he saw one. We saw the aircraft arrive, and the Duke of Kent dressed in a Group Captains uniform came towards us. We were all lined up ready for inspection, I was the third last in the front row, and as he came down the ranks I brought the rifle close to my shoulders and holding my head up, I stuck my chin out in a proud fashion, and the Duke passed me, and retraced his steps and said "You look like a smart airman", I said "Yes, Your Majesty", and then he asked me what my ambitions were in the service and I told him I wanted to be a wireless operator, air gunner, and he also asked me what part of the West Country I came from, and when I replied that I came from Ireland he seemed rather amazed. I was really thrilled to think he had spoken to me, and when I challenged the smart airmen who had criticised me earlier there was no reply forthcoming.

Shortly after this, we went back to Blackpool. We felt that we were really men of battle as we displayed our G.G. badges on our tunics, but a few remarks like being called Girl Guides soon altered our tunes, and we settled down to morse in the Winter gardens in Blackpool. We all liked it at first, but soon it was morse for breakfast dinner and tea and even when you went to the pictures to forget, you were conscious of some overkeen airman tapping out Did it ta, Did it tat on the floor of the cinema. We were fortunate in seeing quite a few celebrities like Anne Ziegler and Webster Booth, Jack Doyle and Movita, Reginald Dixon, and many others.

I tried hard to make a success of the morse but I was getting on fine until

I travelled from Liverpool to Egypt in the H.M.T. Strathaird

Some of the nurses in London

it came to the twelve words a minute test at Burtons and I lost control of myself, so I asked to be released from the course, and to be a straight gunner without the morse. The instructor tried to reason with me, but I felt that if I was in the aircraft and some peoples lives depended on sending the message through correctly, I should not be truthful if I got a message through and tried to cover up for my nervousness at making a mistake.

Thus it was I was posted to Peterhead Airfield in Scotland. I was thrilled at this as I was going to some of the places I had always wanted to go to, but the glamour soon wore off, when I was detailed to take charge of the salvage department on the station. There was no sign of my airgunners course coming through, and I thought how wasteful the RAF were in making me do a job that did not require any intelligence, and I felt I had been cheated. But in the services you do the job and complain later, otherwise the guard room would always be full. I stuck it out for many months making a success of collecting so much salvage in a short time, but deep in my heart I was longing to be back at medical school, in preference to doing the job offered me.

One day a notice appeared on Daily Routine Orders saying there were no more vacancies for air gunners without morse, so I volunteered for overseas service, as I was told there were no medical vacancies except for the W.A.A.F.S. L.A.C. Hart and myself volunteered for overseas and within a very short time we were on our way to Wilmslow in Manchester to await instructions. But I must say that I enjoyed my stay in Peterhead. I went dancing often and I was never short of girlfriends. As a matter of fact, I was nicknamed Smiler in Peterhead, and the Aberdonian sense of humour was certainly proficient.

One morning we were paraded on the barrack square complete with kit bags for destination unknown. All innoculations completed, we received the blessing of the Roman Catholic Padre. We sailed from Liverpool on board H.M.S. Strathaird and joined the convoy which sailed from Glasgow. It was only when we joined the convoy that we realised how large was the British Navy. Everybody was terribly sea sick at first, but we soon settled down having tried sleeping in hammocks. I found that by helping in the sick quarters I could have a mattress on the floor, and I found it more comfortable than sleeping in a hammock.

While I was helping with the teas in the sick bay one day, I was asked by Sister Barnett, an Army Nursing Sister, to give her a hand with blanket bathing a patient. This I was only too delighted to do, and so made known to her my nursing skill as a nurse which she soon observed. She asked where I had trained as a nurse and why I was not in the Medical Corps. I told her that I had tried but was not accepted because they were able to get female nurses. So from that date I was helping her all the time and she even approached the Senior Medical Officer on board ship to get me transferred to the Medical Corps when I landed at my destination. Life was becoming really interesting and one day my opportunity came to special a patient with Sister Barnett. I soon found out that we had a young patient from Brighton with Cerebral

Spinal Meningitis; so it was that I was able to really give my whole heart to specialising this boy with Sister Barnett in charge and F/Lt. Russell in charge of the case. We called first at Freetown and spent a week there. It was lovely to see the native boys diving for their shillings thrown from the side of the ship. The weather was really hot now, a little different from the rain and cold of Wilmslow.

During our voyage out, there was no opportunity for the Roman Catholics on board ship to attend Mass on Sundays as we had no Padre. Other denominations had their Padres to conduct their services, so I took it on myself to organise the Rosary to be said every Sunday by all Roman Catholics, and also a few hymns to be sung. The co-operation I received from the adjutant, looking back on these days, it pays tribute to the high standard of morality held by all ranks on board. We sailed on for several more weeks and what a splendid picture it was to look over the side and see the ships of the convoy spread across the ocean as far as the eye could see, and what a comforting thought it was to have such strength around us. Thank God, we did not get attacked during our journey, but we were always prepared.

I was, of course, still nursing away conscientiously and Sister Barnett was well pleased with the progress of the patient. Many an hour she slept fully clothed just to be near her patient, and I admired her devotion to duty, and was thrilled to be part of that devotion.

As our ship set sail for Durban, one half went to Capetown and the other half of the convoy went with us. So it was that by the time we reached Durban our patient was no longer dangerously ill, and I was chosen to travel ashore with him to the Fever Hospital in Durban where I parted from him with a deep feeling of loneliness. I knew he would be returning to dear old England when he recovered. I had three days in Durban and I was thrilled with the hospitality I received wherever I went. The Victory Club was a great meeting place for all the forces, and we owe a lot to the hospitality of the kind ladies who served us.

One of the things I enjoyed most was the ride I had in the Rick Shaw before I joined the Mauretania and we were all sorry to leave the country we had just got to know.

The first thing I organised on board was to get together again for the Rosary on Sundays, and the Chief Purser Eric Neilson from Liverpool was of great assistance in getting the use of the Catholic Chapel on board for the Roman Catholics.

It was not many days before we landed in Port Said, and the many friends I had made on board during the voyage came to say good byes. Sister Burnett and I, according to reports, were to receive some recognition for our devotion to duty, but I have never received any merit for it. It was nice to know we were able to help in saving life, and what more can anyone ask than to feel satisfied with their work. The two Padres of the other denominations came to say goodbye and they told me they were amazed to think that I had more people at our Rosary than they had combining forces.

We landed ashore with the blazing Egyptian sun burning the backs of our legs and soon we were to be taken to M.E. Pool in the Canal Zone to await transfer to our different units. I was able to get my posting cancelled so that I could remuster to the medical corps and so it was that I did all my exams at that Station and I also got my Hygiene and Sanitation Certificate. Jackie Smalley and myself receiving the highest results in Middle East Command. It is to Paul M. Davies F/LT that I owe my gratitude to because he lectured and assisted me with my examinations. I was on the permanent staff of this unit, and I enjoyed my work immensely although I had several attacks of Dysentery. I also had charge of the skin ward, which I found very interesting. I had occasion while on duty there, of rescuing two burning pilots that crashed within a week of each other. One was dead when Johnny Freeman the Ambulance Driver and I got there. The other was alive but his face was beyond recognition and he died on the ambulance. I shall never forget how disappointed Johnny was because he was not able to get him to hospital. They were both young officers in their early twenties, one of them had only been married a week before flying out from England.

During the time I was on the boat, and the time of my arrival in Egypt, I kept up a steady correspondence with a girl from Stoke-on-Trent and we wrote regularly to each other. Then one day I took a shower and without drying myself I fell asleep on top of my bed. Next morning I was violently sick and the Sergeant was cross as I was not on duty. When he realised what my temperature was he was most apologetic and I was treated for Malaria, but one nursing orderly failed to notice the colour of my sputum and were it not for my own observations I could have been laid to rest in a foreign grave. I told the Medical Officer that I had rusty coloured sputum and I was immediately transferred to 19th British General Hospital. I was immediately visited by the Assistant Matron and the Roman Catholic Padre but it never dawned on me that they were concerned about me. When I had fully recovered I was informed by the Ward Sister that I had Lobar Pneumonia, and that I had been on the danger list for three days. The constant attention I got from these Army Nursing sisters was really marvellous. The only thing I did not like was the sulphonamide drugs they gave me, as I felt so sickly after them. But thank God I was up for Easter Sunday. I helped in the ward, taking temperatures and pulses and I felt sad the day I parted from them all.

They arranged for me to be sent to Telaviv in Palestine for three weeks convalescence. I soon made progress there and I gained the friendship of a German Jewess named Ruth Gitman of the Jewish Services Club. They were very good to all the RAF boys from the camp and they arranged dances and outings for us. Three weeks over I was sent back to my unit, but not for long. I was soon on my way back to Jerusalem to be stationed at the Italian Hospital, which the RAF had taken over there. Of course, I was thrilled to bits because previously I had spent seven days in Jerusalem and knew all the places. I had indeed done a pilgrimage to all the holy places connected with Our Lord's life.

Pictures of very happy times in Egypt

Middle East Air Crew Reception Centre, Egypt

The thought of being stationed there was wonderful, because of my off duty there were so many places to go to and so many people to see. I had many happy months in Egypt and happy memories of the friends I made.

There was one friend in particular whom I will always be grateful to, and that was Madame Godin from Ismailia, who met me one evening for tea, and I was ushered to a lovely spacious room with nice Venetian Blinds. The furniture and the rich tapestries that surrounded me made me feel I was in the house of a great lady. As the tea was brought in by her servants I realised that her mother was the oldest English woman in Egypt, nearly one hundred years old. I was introduced to her that evening. Her memory was accurate, and we talked of politics long before my day, of her part in three wars, and of her famous Polish husband whose name was Kizeinska. She had lived in high society and it was through her connections that her daughter married a brilliant French surgeon in the Canal Zone. I had a long conversation with her mother about the English Royal Family, the different Prime Ministers, General Smuts and so on. It was indeed a privilege to have met such a distinguished lady. Her daughter carried with her, her mother's graciousness, her charm and dignity of movement. Every day off I had from then on, was spent visiting her and it was almost my second home. One evening she asked me to bring some friends to dinner. It was a four course dinner with all the trimmings. Everything went well until the asparagus was brought in and one of these airmen had never seen any before so he started trying to eat it with a knife and fork. I lashed out with my right foot under the table and kicked as hard as I could to catch his eye, so that he could watch me eat it. Then a bowl and cloth were brought in for washing the fingers, and he thought it was some sort of soup. It is with nostalgia that I think of that evening together, as it was one of the happiest evenings we spent in that theatre of war. I had made many friends but in an autobiography of this sort you cannot bring all your individual friends into the limelight.

Another pleasant memory I always retain was the weekend I spent in Cairo after the Hygiene and Sanitation course finished in Almazzo. LAC Smalley and myself went to stay at the Red Shield Club in Cairo but there was no room, so we went to Hibbert House off Soliman Pasha street, and there I made enquiries concerning accommodation, but I found myself on the wrong floor and I spoke to a young lady in front of me seated behind a desk. I made my enquiries and she gave me a rather curt reply, but I was not to be put off so easily. I asked her what part of Ireland she came from, but she informed me that she had attained the Irish accent from her father who came from Athlone, which I then informed her was fifteen miles from my home. She told me that her father did not like her to talk to soldiers. I then proceeded to tell her what I thought of snobbery and that in Ireland we spoke to one and all in a friendly manner. She could see I was annoyed and asked me what my name was and what camp I came from. A week later a card arrived asking me for a weekend in Cairo. All the boys at the camp would not believe it. How ever did you get a date like that they asked because as usual it was very hard to get a date with a girl in Cairo except you were a commissioned officer. I went to Cairo and really enjoyed my weekend. She had a beautiful home and her father was the Editor of the Sphinx magazine. So it only goes to prove that you can make people realise that the scum of the earth is not to be found in the Army or Air Force.

Before I go on to my transfer, I would like to recall my happy days spent at 107 Maintenance Unit with the Dental Officer whom I helped for three months during the absence of his dental orderly. I really learned all I wanted to know about teeth from this gallant officer who was also a great dancer. He taught me the quick-step and slow fox trot when we didn't have patients. He came from the North of Ireland, but the fact that I came from the South did not make any difference to him.

As I look through the pages of my Autograph Book and see the passages that have been written by Jackie Smalley Sgt. Noble RAF, D. Harrison, Cyril Begley, Sean Quilter who went to the same college in County Cork as I had been, and who came from Ballybunion in Kerry. AC Hopkins, LAC Grech from Malta, LAC McGarty RA, Sgt. Leonard, Captain Pollard and many other comrades, it makes me think of the spirit of comradeship that did exist during the war and these trying days. The ENSA shows that were provided for us, the NAAFI girls who were always smiling. The RAF Padre who ministered the rites to all, each to his own denomination, that really no period of civilian life could compare with the spirit of charity that prevailed between Officers and NCOS alike. Of course, there was the odd exception which you will always find to spoil community life. I often feel that I would like to meet and relive these days again, and there is one occasion I can never forget and that was when we were told that Rommel was only so many miles from Alexandria, that we had to have everything prepared to move at a moments notice; how calm everything was done, as if it was daily routine.

Fr. Spunner was our chaplain in the Middle East. He held services and I used to serve his Mass in the NAAFI every Sunday. He was also a great friend. When I was in St. Mel's College he had been playing for St. Finians in Mullingar. He was chucked out of that college he told me, because he was caught smoking too many times. He went off to England, took a course in Theology and educated himself, and became a priest. He went back to the President of St. Finians College in Mullingar who nearly dropped off his seat when he discovered he was a priest. Fr. Spunner said it looked good to see the expression on his face. He used to go down and see the soldiers and spent hours in their tents. He visited the prisoners who were in the guard room and took them cigarettes. I have memories of these people he tried to save, and the people he brought joy to when depressed. He was a very co-operative and friendly person.

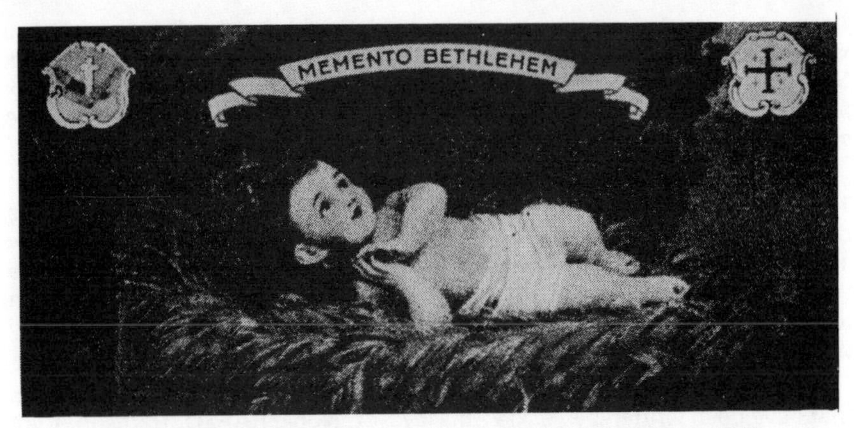

Mid-night Mass St. Catherine's, Bethlehem, Christmas 1943

Myself and friend

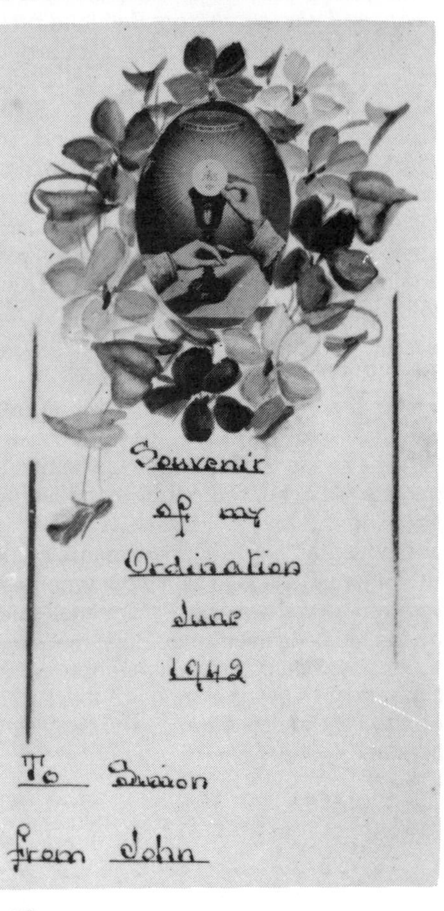

THE READING ROOM

WITH COMPLIMENTS FROM THE MANAGER OF

VIEW FROM ROOF of C.W.L. HOSTEL SHOWING S.W. CORNER of OLD CITY-PLAIN of REPHAIM & CORNER OF NEWER JERUSALEM

The C.W.L. HOSTEL for H.M. FORCES Jerusalem

Fr Austin Treamer, Chaplain to R.A.F. in Jerusalem

The great day arrived when LAC Hamilton and I said good bye to Egypt and moved to Palestine. We wanted, of course to go straight to the Western Desert, but as I had previously enjoyed my leave in charge of the M.I. Room, I was in charge of three small wards, one of which was the Officers ward and Sgt. Leadbeater and F/Lt Bennett were in charge of us. We were a happy bunch and our unit was called the No. 1 Middle East Air Crew Reception Centre. Although the war was in full swing and we had more or less moved away from it, it was one of the happiest units I have ever been in. We soon settled down to routine, and time passed quickly. I spent most of my off duty at meetings in the Catholic Womens League Hostel in the old city. Although the war has been over now many years, the people I used to meet there still have their annual reunion in London every year. Rev. A. Treamer A.A. RAF Chaplain Fr. Curtin of the Fathers of Mount Zion, Sgt. Hodgson, Eileen Hemus one of the WAAF and numerous others. We had "Sword of the Spirit" meetings, "Legion of Mary" and attended most of the Christmas and Easter pilgrimages. We had a wonderful opportunity to see all the places of sanctity from where the very essence of Christianity was founded.

Fr. Treamer was the very best friend I ever had, we had long and useful discussions, advice given freely which was to be a great character formation in the years that followed. One amusing incident I always recalled was going to the Lake of Galilee with Father Mathias and a few other boys. Father and I finished up in a boat on our own and as I tried to row, so the boat went round round but did not go anywhere else. Father shouted "I am not Our Lord you know, who could walk on the waters and I have not got webbed feet", so before I turned him upside down we decided to come back to dry soil again.

I became friendly with a family who lived out near the German Hospice. Mr. and Mrs. Nazzal and their daughter Marian. Marian had married a Palestine Policeman, an Irishman, but some trouble started and Ronnie was discharged, thereby taking up a civilian job with an engineering firm. Some trouble arose there and in the end Ronnie returned to Ireland. I felt sorry for this young couple whose marriage was on the rocks. I do hope that they found themselves again and they settled down together. Marian's family treated me like their own son, and I spent some very pleasant evenings at their house. During this time, I got to know a South African officer who was of Irish descent. One night he took me out to the Snake Club and he dressed me up as a South African Officer, a risky thing to do, I had a lovely time doing the Congo and so on. I danced gaily all evening and didn't worry about the pips on my shoulder. When we returned to the officer quarters of our unit, the orderly officer made some remark to me and I told him it was about time he put the lights out. My own Medical Officer recognised me, but he turned his back and smiled to himself. Still though I was rather merry, I must admit, I certainly took a chance.

About a week later Marian invited me and two other officers to dinner and

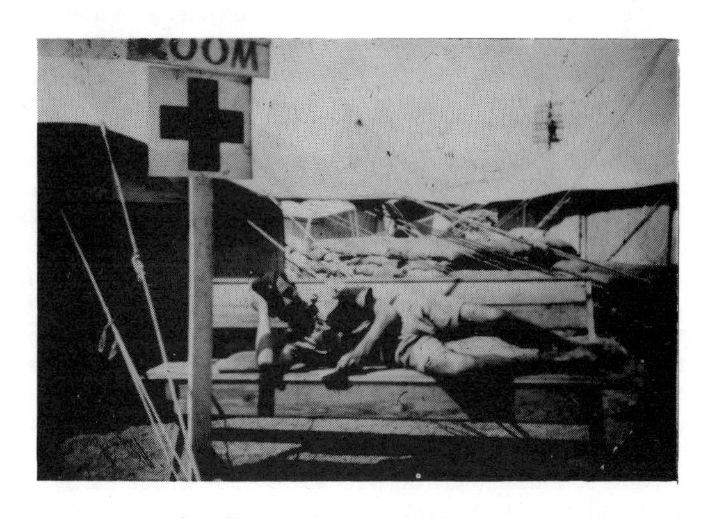

Self on seat when Rommel was only 60 miles from Alexandria

The Church of All Nations in Jerusalem

a wedding anniversary they were having for her brother who had been in the British Army but had got his discharge on medical grounds. He was married to a Chechoslovackian girl who was really charming. The other two officers were unable to attend to Marian's brother and I started drinking after a beautiful meal which had been served by Mrs. Nazzal. We finished a bottle of the Hague Scotch Whiskey, a bottle of French Liqueur and a bottle of Cherry Brandy between us, and I danced like I never danced in my life. Then I started counting everybody who was in the room until someone gave me some salted peanuts and I had no vision of anything else, until I found myself being carried from a taxi by an RAF policeman and the taxi driver throwing water on me to revive me. This policeman carried me and laid me on the medical officers couch to sleep it off. Sgt. Leadbeater took me upstairs to bed, and as he put me to bed I could hear him saying 'Oh dear what are we going to tell the Medical Officer in the morning, he will never believe LAC Corkery was drunk, the only sober man on his staff'. So next morning I was not in a fit state to go on duty and I had to report to his office that afternoon. He gave me a stern lecture about drinking alcohol and how serious it might be, but he was also considerate by telling me that the same happened to him when he passed his examinations as a doctor. I had to do an extra weeks night duty, but that was all the punishment I got.

Christmas 1943 was the one I shall always remember, because I was able to attend the Midnight Mass in Bethlehem, which was indeed a great privilege, and it was not everyone who could attend. Fr. Treamer arranged that all the Catholics from our unit should go and I saw all the representatives of all the countries in Palestine attend this great occasion. Sir Harold McMichael represented the Queen, Eastern Monarchs and so on. After all the aristocracy I saw one of the RAF Air Force walk up calmly and take his seat after all the others. I think all our boys, must have laughed their heads off. The thing that struck me most was when a star appeared above the High Altar, the Franciscan choir sang loud and clear, and Gloria in Excelsis, you felt as if God in all His Majesty had come down among us. Then the procession of the Bambino which was borne by the Patriarch of Jerusalem to the Grotto where it was to lay, it was almost life like and I felt really thrilled. Even now, forty five years later, as I visit a Midnight Mass, my thoughts turn into that joyful occasion, and although I know it is the same Mass and the same sacrifice, I still feel I want to return to Christmas Eve 1943.

One unfortunate incident happened shortly after, in the New Year, which was to put a cloud over my stay in Palestine. I had just finished seven days local leave and had just returned to Haifa, when I called in to see my unit. I noticed there was a light on in the unit Post Office and knocked on the window to see if there was any mail for me. I was sadly disappointed on the Corporal in charge, because he was at that moment ripping up a parcel of cigarettes which had been sent to a sergeant in the unit. Having asked him what he was doing to the parcel, he tried to bribe me with forty cigarettes and I threw them back at him and said good night. Jimmy Hamilton was still up when I arrived in and he must have seen I was really shocked at this stage, and he asked what was wrong. I was loathe to tell him, and when I did he said there was only one thing to do, and that was to report it. Having informed Squadron Leader Bennett our Medical Officer, he insisted I report it to the authorities because he said it was a serious charge and no mail would be safe.

After I reported the facts, all hell broke loose. A few weeks later the Corporal in charge of the Post Office was court martialled and I was chief witness for the prosecution. The officer defending the Corporal was an Australian and he was a brilliant lawyer. By the time I had been cross examined I felt I was the criminal and I never relaxed until the whole thing was over. He was reduced to the ranks and got one hundred and twenty days field punishment, and having been passed medically fit for his punishment by our medical officer he was again made run round the parole ground by the Army Medical Officer who discovered he had a murmur of the heart. I was relieved to hear it and the irony of the whole thing was that he was sent back to our unit and I had to be his medical escort in the ambulance. I felt terrible inwardly, but I heard afterwards he was discharged from the forces on medical grounds and did not have to serve his sentence. So in a way I did him a favour, his four friends were looking for me in Jerusalem that night and I was really worried but I heard later that they were posted to different units and I was airborne to Sicily next day. So ended a chapter in my life that I do not wish to recall.

I flew from Cairo to Benghazi to Tripoli — to Tunis and then to Naples and Sicily. It was a wonderful flight and I looked forward to making new friends. I was sorry to say good-bye to LAC Hamilton and F/Lt Bennett but such is war, here today and in twenty four hours in a different theatre of war. The allied invasion had pushed on past Sicily at this time and I soon found my way around. I had to do twenty four hours ambulance duty at the airfield at Catania and the Corporal and other LAC shared the duties of the sick bay. I liked it on the airfield. We did our own cooking and with Mount Etna in the background it was a really happy unit. Then one day I was approached by an airman to meet a Sicilian girl named Maria Ursino. She was taking her degrees in foreign languages at Catania Uniersity, this was during the first few months of 1944. Maria was a very attractive girl and spoke English very well. She had been taught by a Welsh airman who was a school teacher in civilian life. I did my best to converse with her and I spent almost all my free evenings with her mother and herself. Her mother was very nice and she sat at one side of the table and Maria on the other. It was a Sicilian custom that girls were always chaperoned by their parents. I did learn that her father had been killed by an RAF raid on the harbour in Naples, but her father was an officer in the Italian Navy. We became very good friends and I found myself falling in love with her. One evening when the mother left to get me a glass of home made wine, Maria started playing the piano, and I held her left hand in mine while she played with her right. I heard her mother shout something in Italian from the other room. Maria explained to me that her mother wanted to know why she was not playing with both hands, so that put an end to holding hands, for the time being at least.

The RAF used to pull my leg about an Irishman teaching a Sicilian girl English when I could not speak English properly myself, so they thought. Our friendship became more serious and my duties were performed quickly at camp so that I could get away to see Maria.

Then out of the blue word came that I was to be posted back to Egypt, as I was the only qualified medical orderly who had passed a Hygiene and Sanitation course in Egypt in 1942 and there had been two cases of Diptheria in RAF in Luxor Upper Egypt. My Medical Officer was very understanding and he did his best to stop the transfer, he was sympathetic himself as he was going steady with an Italian girl who worked in the orderly room. I broke the news to Maria and we decided to get engaged. I went all over Catania but it was impossible to get a gold ring anywhere, so I purchased a silver ring with an Aqua Marine Stone. I went to meet Maria and she was overjoyed, and her mother was pleased, but not so her sister, who slapped her across the face and asked her had she forgotten that it was the RAF who had been responsible for her father's death. Anyhow, we became engaged on the 16th October 1944, and I flew by way of Malta where I had breakfast, to Algiers, about five and a half direct hours flying. I landed at an American airfield in Algiers where I stayed for three days.

There was another English airman with me who was flying to Egypt as well. He was an RAF Corporal and we went out to the Cabaret a couple of nights. We were sitting at a table enjoying a beer one night when someone called out is there a medic in the house, and having seen my medical badges I was rushed to the ladies toilet where a girl had passed out. I tried reviving her at first by putting her head down and massaging the back of her neck, and then I tried putting a wet sponge down her back which had an immediate effect. She came to, and put her arms around me and nearly smothered me. There was a great laugh from all the American boys, but her boyfriend was not too pleased. Feeling very much the hero of the night, we went out again on the last night of our stay. Patrick O'Brien the American film star flew in after entertaining the troops. I had the pleasure of meeting him. I said "Good morning Pat". He said "That is no way for an Irishman to address another Irishman"! He told me I should say "The top of the morning to you Pat", and that the answer should be "Sure and the rest of the day to yourself".
So that was one greeting I will never forget. We had a great chat, and we boarded the plane for home. I gave him my Irish Rosary and he was delighted with it. I hoped that one day I would have the pleasure of meeting him again.

We flew from Algiers to Tripoli, Tripoli to Tunis, and then to Cairo where we boarded a train from Cairo arriving at Luxor. This was a small unit, one officer, twenty-five airmen, one American officer and about twenty American airmen and an Army anti-malaria unit. There was no medical officer except for Captain Mann, the Army Medical Officer who came in to see us from time to time. We had an old retired Egyptian Medical Officer who was in the British Army in the first world war, and he was a very interesting gentleman named Dr. Shakael Farhma, who we would get in an emergency, but it did mean that time was lost sending transport for him. So my responsibilities were varied. I had the usual RAF medical returns to do.

Having made myself known to all parties I went round checking up on the Hygiene and Sanitation of the camp. I had an Egyptian helper in the sick bay who was quite intelligent. He kept calling me Dr. Paddy and tried to tell me everything was OK. Dr. Taiffee had inspected everything before he left. He was a nice lad but I came up with nothing for a few weeks until I got a call from flying control tower that something funny was going on in the camp perimeter so with the aid of a pair of binoculars, we were able to detect some natives burying or throwing something away.

I found out from my native helper Hasum Hussein that this was his uncle who had the contract for burying refuse from the kitchens so I ordered a 15 cwt van and we tore along the airport to see for ourselves. Before long we discovered that not only were they burying the refuse in shallow pits but also the bandages and dirty dressings that should be burnt or buried six feet were covered by about eighteen inches of sand and easy to be taken away at night and the bandages sold to the natives in the huts. I ordered him to dig the hole six feet deep and he stayed there until he was able to stand in it to his full height. Hasum, his nephew, explained to him that I would take his contract away if he did not bury everything six feet down and then to wash his hands thoroughly afterwards.

I sent a report of what was happening, and all airmen who had been visiting native villages to meet girls were stopped from going there. So it is possible that the two airmen who died from Diptheria were infected by the company they were keeping.

I got very strict, not only with all the natives employed, but with our own RAF cadets etc. I became unpopular and at one stage having had all pets destroyed because of directions from Cairo, that I had only a few friends left at the Camp. Mr. Paterson, the Commanding Officer backed me up to the hilt, and having kept the camp sickness down to a minimum, I gained their confidence once more, and I was admired for the discipline I kept.

I was very successful in transferring RAF personnel to Cairo by air at all stages, as the boys in flying control would contact any aircraft flying up from the Red Sea to land and take the patients direct to RAF hospital at Cairo. We became a very happy and efficient unit and even though I had no relief medic I was happier than I had expected to be. I wrote several times to Maria, but communication was slow and it was through an Italian nun in Cairo that I kept in contact. Apparently she became very unhappy at my parting and it was affecting her studies. I nearly succeeded in getting a transfer back to Catania when Squadron Leader Dickie recognised my name on the transfer list and there was hell to play, and the poor sergeant who tried his best to get my posting was in hot water himself.

Then I got Seborrhoea of the Scalp from the showers I was taking to keep cool as it was 120 degrees in the shade. I had to see a skin specialist. I started losing my hair so it was decided that I should be transferred to a cooler climate.

Before I go on with my story, I would like to make the record straight regarding Maria. I had a letter from an Italian nun in Cairo who told me that Maria was having trouble studying and she advised me to release her from our engagement. Other people advised me also, they told me it would be difficult to get a position in Italy after the war, and also that our different customs might cause problems in our marriage. As a matter of fact we did have an understanding about it, so she decided to keep my ring as a mark of our friendship. It was difficult to make this decision, but as I could not go back there, it was better to separate. We wrote to each other for many years afterwards. She finished her studies in Catania. Her command of the English language was marvellous, I felt honoured that I had in some way helped her to speak it better.

I got posted to Greece in the summer of 1945. I was posted to 107 Staging Post Transport Command. I feel at this stage I must tell you that Eddie McCord joined the Royal Air Force and he was a trained air gunner on a training course. For going into action he passed his morse course and he felt so proud that where I had started out to do the same thing, Eddie had passed all before him. His plane crashed in a night exercise somewhere over England. I wrote to his mother sympathising with her and in July 1943 I received a long letter from her telling me that she was broken hearted. It is one letter I have kept over the years as I was such a great friend of Eddie's. 'Lord have mercy on him'. His sister Phyllis joined the WAAF and she was posted to Europe. I had a long letter from her when I was in Athens.

Fr. John, my brother, was ordained in 1942 in our own church in Ardagh. I was the only member of the family absent. He sent me a lovely hand painted card for myself and having taught in the St. Mels College, he went out in the missions to Nigeria as head of the ABAK College. He had attained several degrees by this time; M.A. B.Sc. S.T.L. D.D. Higher Diploma in Education. Now you will realise how difficult it was for me to follow a genius. He wrote regularly, and so did Daddy, whose second family grew to eleven in all.

I found myself flying more than I walked in Athens. My duties were that of Medical Escort to patients to and from the islands of Salonica and Rhodes, and bringing them to the Army Hospital in Athens. It was a lovely change from Luxor in Egypt and my skin condition improved. There was plenty of female company to be had, but although some were very friendly and nice, the war had left its mark on these people and food was very scarce, so that members of the forces were vulnerable as regards satisfying their needs.

Prostitution was rampant in all the streets. Such are the horrors of war as it progresses. Hunger, poverty and the black market lowered the moral standard of the population, but who are we to judge, we are all God's creatures and His love for them is probably greater because of their physical wants. The same could be seen in Sicily and the countries that were rescued by the allies.

In the meantime I started writing to a girl whose name was given to me as a pen friend. As the months passed, the war was now coming to a climax. I began writing seriously to her. Frances was her name.

I really enjoyed my transfer to Greece. Swimming was available, the night life in Athens was beginning to pick up and you could go to the opera. I went to see the Acropolis. Athens is so full of history from the time of St. Paul to the present day; her people are a brave people through history. They have had so many invasions and yet survived. They were loyal to England and they are a trusting people. I was very happy and I enjoyed flying duties.

One day I was asked to fly with a head injury to Bari in Naples. I had seven days leave coming to me, so I arranged to have it in Rome. I arranged to fly my patient to Bari and from there to Naples, and then on to Rome. It was a pleasant journey. I took off at about 10 a.m., arriving in Bari around lunch time. There was an ambulance waiting there to meet me. I got a flight to Naples and then to Rome, having delivered my patient safely Thank God, as I was on the permanent staff of Transport Aircraft going through. I just went to the booking office and I was made welcome to all their centres.

The flight to Bari was pleasant except that we got into air pockets, which meant we suddenly lost height on two occasions. I was holding on to my stomach muscles and holding on to my patients hand as steady as I could. On arrival in Rome, I made my way to the Catholic Women's League Club for service men and women. I booked in for my seven days. I served Mass the second morning I was there. I met a fine looking lady who had served Mass that morning and she said I could carry on any morning I wanted. Having had breakfast with her, we had a long chat about Ireland, Athens and London before the war. She was a well spoken lady. She told me she had spent summer holidays in England. I remember saying to her "You're old man must be well off to let you have holidays in England". And one of the other ladies overheard me and laughed and told me I was in the company of Countess Ursino a member of the Italian Royal family who was dressed in a C.W.L. uniform. She never let on, and I was asking her about getting a gold chain in Athens for a friend in London as I had a gold Jerusalem Cross which I had attained in Jerusalem. She said she would get me one, and it only cost one pound. The ladies told me afterwards that gold chains are almost impossible to get and that it was probably one of her own pieces of jewellery. She was nice to talk to. No one would believe she was a countess, although her dignity was obvious.

I had occasion to meet Monsignor Hugh O'Flaherty, who was in charge of the Popes affairs, and he was a Killarney man. He took me to his private apartment which was overlooking St. Peter's Square and he slept right over the quarters that were originally used by the Pope as they were over the vault of St. Peter's tomb. He told me of a price that was on his head by the Germans for delivering airmen through the Vatican and through the Irish Ambassador who got them safely back to England. General Alexander offered him the highest award the king could bestow for risking his life in securing the safety of British airmen out of Italy during the occupation by the Germans. I had a meeting with Delia Murphy the wife of the Irish Ambassador at a dinner given at the Augustinian

House in Rome and Fr. O'Connor and myself were introduced to the two American Officers and it was at this dinner that I learned of Delia Murphy's exploits in helping to use the Irish Embassy as a safe haven for the airmen. It was a beautiful meal and the wine served from decanters was their own wine from the vineyard. We had a great night and Fr. O'Connor and myself left to go back to the Hostel. He managed to get in some way but I had to go back to the Augustinian House and seek refuge for the night. My punishment was I was called at 6 a.m. to serve Mass on St. Patrick's altar for the priest. I signed my name on the Visitor's Book and it was about thirty names below that of Eamonn De Valera. I visited the Alecander Club in Rome, and I then paid a guide a pound an hour to see all the places of interest in the Vatican. I was very fortunate to see the Sistine Chapel, the roof of which took Michael Angelo four and a half years to paint — every scene from Adam and Eve to judgement day is recorded. You could spend hours in the catacombs, the private vestments of various Popes. I met an Irish Christian Brother who did all the Pope's book binding and we had a public audience with Pope Piux XII on December 8th, 1945. This is a day I will remember for the rest of my life. He walked so quickly into the audience room and he spoke in English and Polish and other languages. He looked a very holy man, and he blessed any objects of piety, and wished us a speedy return home to our loved ones, and he prayed that we should convey his greetings to our family and friends. I wore the cross of honour I had received from the Custodian guardian of the Holy Sepulchre when I visited the Holy places on three different occasions. I was so overjoyed that I spent the next few days visiting and looking at the Palace of Victor Emmanuel. Certain quarters were out of bounds to airmen because of the risk they ran of being robbed in the alley ways. Starvation of the people was obvious to see, the black market was in full swing.

My grandmother died with the crucifix I sent her in her hands. She never let it go all the years she lived 'Lord have mercy on her'. My memories of that week are as vivid today as they were on the 8th December, 1945.

On my return journey from Rome I got in an airplane that had left London in the morning, direct to Rome and direct to Athens via Adriatic Sea, Ionian Sea, the Island of Corfu, Gulf of Corinth — Athens. I spoke to some people who told me of the way life was returning to normal back in England.

CHAPTER V

There is one incident I must record and that was that I was admitted to the RAF Hospital in Cairo for an Adenoidectomy, because the ENT Specialist Squadron leader McKenzie realised I was left with a nasal infection from the time of my illness in Egypt in 1942. I was operated on in the morning of May 6th 1945, and on the afternoon of May 7th the war with Germany finished and all nurses all over the hospital were celebrating the victory. We could hear the cheering in London on the radio and it was a great relief. I was still feeling rather weak after my operation, but I tried to get out of bed, and walked towards the Sister and we went out on the lawn to dance, I in my pyjamas. I started off fairly well but after a few turns I was flat on my back with the Sister trying to hold on to me. It was a hilarious three days of celebrations. One sergeant who had too much to drink could not find his way back to the ward, but walked in to a hut and finding an empty bed fell asleep on it. Next morning he awoke to the shouts and screams of twenty females, as he had slept in one of the WAAF huts all night. I'm sure it was the talk of the hospital. He was not punished as he was an acclaimed hero. I recovered and went for a few days to Jerusalem to recuperate and saw most of my old friends. Everywhere seemed different; everyone was talking about returning home and I was asked by a nursing sister to bring her back a fur coat. She gave me forty pounds to get one. They were very cheap there. I travelled to Telaviv, which was then beginning to take shape, and went on a sight-seeing tour. I had two years ago, written my name in Gaelic in the visitors book in the Jewish Services Club. I could safely say that mine was the first name to be recorded there. I went to the airfield and succeeded in getting a seat in a privately owned four seater light aircraft. It belonged to one of the Commanding Officers in the RAF who was flying back to Egypt. It was a pleasant flight back, and we landed at RAF airfield in Heliopolis in Cairo. There was only one question worrying me, and that was how I could get through customs with a woman's fur coat. I had another airman with me who suggested that I wear it under my winter coat. It looked odd, but I was so thin I got away with it, by telling the RAF police that I had permission to wear it due to my years in the hot climates, especially having been in Luxor where it was one hundred and twenty degrees in the shade. I got to the Catholic Women's League Club, met my friend, and got taken out to tea with her. This was a very pleasant evening, one of my last in Cairo. I was airborne to Athens next day.

I was awarded the Cross of honour from the Holy Sepulchre by the Custodian Guardian of the Holy Sepulchure, by the Franciscian Father who travelled with us on tours of the Holy Land and as I had made three visits there I was given that privilege. It is a great honour and you are entitled to wear it in audience with the Holy Father or in a Corpus Christi procession. It was the same honour awarded to Crusaders in the old days of chivalry, to record their merits. I did wear that decoration when I had a public audience with Pope Pius XII on the 8th December, 1945. I settled down to routine duties again, and now several people on the camp were preparing for their return to Blighty as they called it. All the married ones who had done three years overseas were entitled and all single men who had done four years were also due to return.

My time was drawing near. I spent a lot of my spare time visiting a club in Athens where I met one of the hostesses. It was actually at a Christmas party at the club I was helping her and she said, "How is it that you are always so happy and full of life". So I got invited to her home to meet her family. I liked her immensely and invited her to a dance at Camp which was a well organised one. Her command of the English language was fantastic. We danced beautifully together and we found we had a lot in common. She was a Roman Catholic. Once again I felt that my feelings for her were getting stronger and although I was writing to Frances at this time, I felt that I could easily settle in Greece. She told me her father owned a large tract of land in Central Africa and that I had no need to return. She said that I could not express an opinion about a girl through writing to her. I went to a party at her house after Christmas and saw in the New Year with her family. It was so different there. They don't celebrate the New Year like they do in Scotland or England. I spent a night there and she stole out of her bedroom to come to my room to kiss me goodnight, having waited for her mother to go to sleep. I knew at this time that my posting back to England would be in about two or three weeks. She tried to change my mind about going back and I was finding it rather difficult myself. I was welcomed by her family but with the experience of Maria still fresh in my thoughts I felt that my future was in England or Ireland. The nights she came to the camp to the dance, we were going home by taxi and when I tried to kiss her she told me it was not a Greek custom. But I put my arms around her and kissed her before she realised it and then I told her that was an Irish custom.

As I look back I cannot but remember all the friends I made of all nationalities. There is no doubt in my mind but that God had endowed me with gifts of tolerance and romance and should I say dreamer. They were gifts that were to be my standby in the years of nursing that lay ahead. I enjoyed our visits to the Opera and Concerts and the sights of Athens. It was such a change from Cairo now that the war had finished. All the talk was about going home and about where we would be posted. Wing Commander Mumby was Commanding Officer and Squadron Leader Kelleher from Macroom was our Medical Officer. In the early part of January 1946 we all lined up on the airfield in Athens and I said goodbye to my many friends and airmen. We were flown in a large transport aircraft which had been fitted out for carrying troops and we were flown to Naples. We were standing side by side in the bottom of the plane where we could see daylight and we could also see that at the touch of a buttom we could have been dropped as the bombs were dropped over Germany. Our hearts were in our mouths. After a meal we set off for Milan where we stayed for two nights and then through the Swiss Alps by train and through France until we sailed from Calais to Dover. It was a pleasant journey. As we went through customs, people were caught bringing souvenirs such as revolvers and they were all confiscated. One airman about four feet high, carried a suitcase bigger than himself and asked one of the military police to carry it, which he did, and walked straight through customs. When we got on the train at Dover and when he opened his case he had revolvers, watches, jewellery and God knows what else. As we reached England on to Victoria, the green fields, the orchards and the green trees looked a pretty picture after four and a half years of sandy beaches, desert sands and rocky country, it seemed like we were being reborn.

We were posted to RAF Kirkham in Lancashire and after a nice wash and rest we were sorted out and I was put in charge of Admissions and Discharges in RAF Kirkham Military Hospital. I had my own office and two WAAF Orderlies working for me. I said I would prefer to work in the wards, but I was told that I had done my share of hard work and that my experience in medical records abroad was needed in the office. I had some leave coming to me so I went to see Frances Boucher who was by this time writing steadily. She knew all about Maria, they had been writing to each other. I spent my leave at her home where I got a great welcome. Her sister Mary was very nice to me too. It was actually Mary who gave me France's address. She was friendly with the girl from Stoke on Trent who stopped writing when I was in Palestine as she met a sailor and married him. People lived from day to day during the war. Whatever was destined for you by God was accepted. I got engaged to Frances and we were very happy.

Dear Aunt Maud

CHAPTER VI

I went back to Longford to see the family. They were all grown up and now living in Longford opposite St. Mels Cathedral. Baby had her hands full with such a large family to contend with. Michael was a fine lad and a great help to Daddy. Molly was working in Longford, she was courting Noel McGeeney. Daddy was pleased to see me. Kathleen, Celene, Philomena and Angela were all at different ages.

Things were very scarce and I went into a shop in Longford and asked for a nice crêpe de chine frock. I gave the lady the measurements. When she asked me her waist measurement I told her it was the length of my arm. She laughed heartily. I purchased the dress and put it away with my other souvenirs. When Daddy came into the house that evening he said where had I been? I said I had been up town. He said "About the length of my arm I suppose". I knew then that he had been told what I had said. It must have been all over Longford the next day. The one I missed on my return visit was Baby's mother. Not to see her sitting by the fire with her stick was a loss to me. Daddy and I understood each other better now, I think we had a profound respect for each other. He had been getting an allowance from the RAF since I went to Sicily. I had to contribute towards it. He told me that the Air Ministry official who came to see him was a gentleman and whereas his profession as a teacher kept his children from availing of scholarships Fr. John had passed his and he was not to avail of it because of Daddy's profession. The number of children he had was not taken into account, but the Air Ministry official was very understanding and he was granted an allowance for me. I visited all my friends in Derrymore and Ardagh. They wanted to know all about my travels in Egypt and how lucky I was to get through the war. They even knew I had been dangerously ill in Egypt. I heard from Daddy that two messages had come from the war office, one to say that I was dangerously ill and one to say that I had a speedy recovery. Daddy was having Masses said for me everywhere. The Padre who visited me in hospital told me that he knew my father. He was the Chaplain who sent the messages and Daddy told me he had been to Loch Derg with this Priest on two pilgrimages. God's will works in many ways. I was dined and wined in all the country houses I went to, and I felt that if I had any more eggs and meat etc. that I would burst; such was the hospitality I received. Kathleen was a very religious, very out-going person. I was not surprised. She was accepted in Our Lady of Mary Order in Castlecor, Ballymahon, Convent as a novice. All that family were a delight and highly intelligent. They were all very successful in examinations. Michael blossomed out as a great soccer player, as goalie for Longford Town and later a goalie for Mayo Football Team, until he received an injury to his back and having had a big operation on it, he went to America with the Mayo Football Team. He was indeed the back-bone of the family during those years. He was a Post Office Engineer.

On my return to England I visited Aunt Maud in Chatham, who was not as friendly towards me as she had been before I went abroad. She looked very old indeed, the war had left its mark on her. The V bombs which Hitler had rocketed to the shores of England had travelled directly over her house and often she had to travel to the hospital at night to make up drugs or medicines badly needed. It was an awkard area for a lady travelling alone without transport and in complete darkness. I gained her confidence after a few days. She was glad to hear of my travels and she was proud of having me accompany her in uniform. She gained the respect of her neighbours and friends at the hospital. She took me to London shopping and we went to Theatres and Restaurants like she used to do in the old days. A priest whom I had met in Palestine had written to her about me and had given her a good account of me. I think that was the turning point. She got angry with me for taking out a girl from Northern Ireland. She had given me some spending money and I spent it on a nice frock for the girl, who was a nurse at the Royal Hospital for Incurables. I had a date with Betty and Aunt Maud wanted to go shopping with me, so she left London for Chatham without speaking to me. This happened during a weeks holidays from the RAF before I went abroad. It was for this reason I was in the bad books. She said that I was discharged from the services I should go back to Cork to see Lily May and bring her to England nursing as no one was taking interest in her. I went back to RAF Kirkham and continued my duties as before. At weekends I travelled to Manchester to see Frances. I met a WAAF in the same office as myself and she was an O'Brien Corkery. She was from Kerry, where my grandfather had originated from.

For many years my Aunt Maud and Aunt Madge always put O'Brien before Corkery — O'Brien Corkery and my sister Lily May had it put on her birth certificate. Uncle Michael had registered my name and I was plain Corkery. Fr. John had it on his certificate as well, my father also used it when he married first. It was on my mother's headstone in Ardagh but somewhere along the line it was gradually dropped. It is a great name in Kenmare. It is very prominent in the Church itself and I have heard my relations say that Daniel Corkery was related to us. Another story told is that O'Brien was the real name and we were O'Briens of Cork and Kerry, hence the name Corkery. Another theory is that we were descended from Lord Inchiquin and my Aunt Maud's house was named Gleninchiquin and another theory was that after the Spanish Armada failure to invade England; a lot of boats put into Kinsale and other places along the coast, and that we were descended from a Spanish family who settled in the area. I have followed some of the family history and found that my grandfather was the first school master in Ballygurteen school and before that school was built he was what was called a hedge school master. He lost charge of Ballygurteen school and Miss McSweeney got it instead. School teaching has followed in our family and probably will continue to do so. I have introduced some family history here because my grandfather died at a very young age, and my grandmother was left with six children — Neilius, Kathleen, Maud, Daddy, Michael and Madge.

One hot summers day in Ballygurteen, the McCarthys were bringing in the hay and saving the harvest and my grandmother called her children together.

She told them she had no money, but they had a harvest and that was, the brains God gave them, and their books if they used them wisely. Each one of her children got on well. Nelius was in the British Civil Service and later in Fords in Cork where he became one of the directors. Daddy was headmaster of his own school in Longford, having attained first place in Ireland. Uncle Michael also became a teacher. Aunt Kathleen also passed for teaching, but had to stay and look after the MacSweeney in Ballinavar. Aunt Maud became a nurse and later a Pharmacist and worked with a doctor in France. She was the first person to lecture on sheep gut which was used in operations during and after World War One. Aunt Madge, highly educated looked after us. So from humble beginnings the Corkerys were noted for their advance in learning through strictness and hard work, and their achievements have been carried forward into todays world. They have not been mentioned in the books of West Cork because they were brought up like that, and as the pages of history are written it is only right and proper that his generation should not be passed over without giving them the tribute they deserve and for their example, friendship, and intelligence, which they shared across the world. Master Madden, who has passed away (Lord have mercy on him) is the man to whom the Corkerys owe their successes. He recognised their talents and it was to him that Daddy, Uncle Michael and Uncle Nelius owe such credit and also to the De la Salle Order in Waterford where they were trained for teaching. They have earned their heavenly reward. I hope that the few words I have attributed to my grandmother is a fitting memorial to a brave woman who faced the odds on that summer in Ballygurteen long ago. She was humble, but dignified; one of those who in the middle of poverty shine forth like a bright star to bring lustre to Gods creation in his likeness. May they all rest in peace.

Having returned to England I had a lot of trouble with my sinuses and I had to have wash-outs regularly. I had to go to the RAF Hospital in Wheaton. I was running a high temperature for a week, so I had to go on Penecillin. I spent about three weeks there altogether. While I was there I had a visit from the Adjutant at RAF Station Kirkham, who wanted me to sign on to the RAF for another five years. I could have been a corporal immediately, with a view to becoming a Sergeant in six months. He also told me that I could apply to be a State enrolled Nurse as I had attained the examinations necessary to qualify, and I could sit for my SRN Examination within one year. This was a great challenge. Both ideas were to be considered. Frances was anxious I should leave the service and finish my training in a Civilian Hospital. I was given two weeks to consider it. Had I been offered promotion in the service earlier, it would have convinced me to stay in, as I really liked the service. I made up my mind to leave the service, I enjoyed going for weekends to Blackpool with Frances as I knew I would go back to Ireland for a long holiday before going back to my nursing career again. At last in June 1946, I was posted to RAF Station Hednesford, and I was medically examined.

After five and a half years I was getting ready for my discharge from the RAF. I got excellent references, and with my Demob suit under my arm I went to Frances's house on 7th June 1946. After a few days, I left to go to Longford and after a week in Longford Daddy advised me to go down to Uncle Michael in Rossmore. Daddy did not have much room as his young family were enough for anyone and finances were not too good for him at this time. My arrival in Cork was great, everyone welcomed me home. Uncle Michael was married and had one little girl called Josephine. Lily May and Aunt Madge were delighted to see me. I went around visiting all my friends; everyone told me I had not changed and that I looked as young as ever. I took a great interest in the Parish and became a great friend of Father James O'Donovan. Mick and Danny Donovan were brothers and they looked after the farm for Michael. As the days went on I felt really relaxed and enjoyed my uncles company. Lily May and I went cycling to Clonakilty and Dunmanway and soon I forgot all about England and I felt very much at home. The weeks turned to months. I had my own money from the RAF. I wrote to Frances often but I could tell by her letters that she was lonely. I felt that I was pressurised to come back and look for a position in a hospital. I tried to tell her that I would like to bring Lily May back nursing to England with me. It would not be easy as she would have fare, papers etc. and I could see that Lily May was very attached to Rossmore. I also felt that her presence was coming between Michael and his wife. I was gradually winning her over. Meanwhile, Frances was getting rather impatient. Finally, I made up my mind that I should break our engagement. I did not like doing this, but I felt that I wanted Lily May settled and myself sorted out. I broke off my engagement with Frances and began organising for Lily May to come over with me. Everyone in Rossmore said I would never take her away.

In the meantime, I made the most of my new found freedom and I went cycling a lot on my own. One weekend I was invited to Schull where there was a sister in the war who had come home to take up this position as matron. It was a beautiful spot, I got introduced to another Nurse who was a night nurse there. I stayed there that night and Teresa and I had a long chat about her training in England. We met several times after this. She was a lovely girl with a wonderful disposition. She went to the Erinville Hospital in Cork and succeeded in getting her mid-wifery certificate. My uncle was delighted that I had met an Irish girl and I felt pretty happy about it myself.

I sang at public concerts in Rossmore, and Father O'Donovan introduced me as the flying airman on a flying visit. I played many tricks on Mrs O'Brien of Rossmore also Mrs. Mitchell, until one day Lily May was calling the men to dinner and Uncle Michael was up in the fields. Lily May caught the front of her right shin on an iron gate with spikes and I actually had to lift her off the spike. We had to take her to Dr. Neville in Clonakilty. It was a nasty gash and was sore for a long time after.

Uncle Michael had the Station while I was there, and that was the first time Mass had been said in the house, and it was owned previously by Harry Good, a Protestant. Lily May had at last made up her mind, and she applied for a position as a nurse in Moorfields Eye Hospital in London. She went to Cork and having completed her application form, she was successful in getting a position. Although she had only primary education, the matron was very well pleased. I paid her fare over, and got her some new clothes to travel with etc. We went to visit our old friends with Aunt Madge. Aunt Madge was really beginning to feel lonely, and as the days grew nearer you could see she was going to miss her alot. Although there was a great understanding between them they did not always hit it off. The age barrier was not healthy for Lily May, who had all her young life in front of her. She had worked so hard on Michael's farm, that I was told she could do the work of three other people.

One evening Lily May and I went to the pictures in Dunmanway, to see the Bells of St. Marys. We really enjoyed it and started for home as it was lighting up time. We started cycling home, and must have taken a wrong turning, as Lily May recognised some sort of a stone monument on the side of the road. I stood on it and tried to shout in the direction of a farm house some distance off the road. She was shouting and hysterical by now and started saying the Rosary in the middle of the road. I wanted to turn back and get our bearings, but no way would she go and said three people had been killed on that stretch of road. A man had been killed on this spot by the Black & Tans during the troubles. It was nearing midnight and a man told us we were on the road to Ballinacarriga. My bicycle was punctured so we walked to Ballinacarriga wheeling the bicycles. We came to the line road home through Ballygurteen and landed home at six o'clock in the morning. Lily May was very frightened and the story was all round Rossmore. Father O'Donovan said we were lucky to have escaped as he had heard many stories about that place, and that somebody had been praying for us. I visited places all round the coast that I never had the privilege of seeing during my childhood. We travelled a lot. We went to a funeral in Kerry, one of the last of the Corkerys, married to the Sullivans in Bonane Road, Kenmare had passed away R.I.P. She was probably my grandfather's sister. We went with Uncle Michael and Aunt Madge. I wish I had taken more notice of the church etc at the time because now I could do with that information, and the people who could help me have all passed away.

CHAPTER VII

In January 1947 we left Rossmore. We spent the night in Cork. Lily May had to travel with other girls who were all going to various places. They had to be examined in Dublin. This was because they were supervised by the Ministry of Labour and had to be examined to see if they had any body lice etc. I objected strongly to this degrading step, and I told the authorities what I thought. They were treated like a lot of cattle for export from the country, and if this was to happen now they would have been brought before the Court of Human Rights at the Hague. Thank God I was able to look after her on the boat and the rest of the journey. We called to see Uncle Nelius in Cork who gave her some money for the journey. He was very fond of her because of the way she looked after his mother. He wished her all the best and told her she was doing the right thing in being independent. The parting from Rossmore was a sad one. The people could not believe it. She was loved by all and even now, so many years later, she is still spoken about. Thus, in a chapter of history, the last of three little children who came to Ballygurteen many years before, was starting her career in nursing in a strange land — strange to her, as she had not travelled far in her lifetime. I felt happy that at last I had fulfilled my promise to Aunt Maud — to take her to England. Aunt Madge, Muriel and Josephine were very lonely after her, as was Uncle Michael. I thought of my first crossing from Holyhead so many years before. What a strange life is destined for us all, when you think of it. I said good-bye to Teresa and promised to write often, although Teresa wanted me to return home again when I could. After a long and tiresome journey we landed in London and I took Lily May to the hospital, before I tried the Salvation Army Hostels, where I used to go when I was in the forces, but somehow it was very hard to get in. Lily May and I tramped the streets Saturday and Sunday until I found a place in Russell Square and I got a nice room there, which was to be my home for a long time to come. The matron was very nice. She was a married lady and a very understanding person. She told my sister after the interview, that she had a job to offer me if I was interested. She had heard that I had been in the Medical Corps and she told me I would be the first male nurse in England to have my Moorfields Eye Certificate, and she would arrange lectures for me. I started civilian nursing again. We were working in the same ward. Lily May looked very smart in her uniform, and she soon became very popular. Sister Davis, a Welsh sister, was in charge of the male wards and I was given all the injections to do as they developed a great deal of confidence in me. I got on well with the Sister but not so with Charge Nurse Russell, who seemed to dislike me intensely. She was always getting on to me, I was glad to see her go off duty. The patients were very cheerful and I had a great way with them. She was jealous of the way they placed their confidence in me. Lily May was put in another ward as Sister thought she was under my influence. I did not need to worry about her; she was very well liked by staff and patients alike, and was very capable in her tests and lectures. The Matron told me that Lily May was far more intelligent than all the nurses who had got their matriculation etc.

I nursed away, but I had a letter from the Ford Motor Company in Dagenham to say Uncle Nelius had written to one of the Directors to get me a job there, where the money was better. I was told to come for an interview. I asked the matron's permission to attend the interview. She was furious and said "Corkery, you are a born nurse, I have had great reports about you". As a matter of fact I had specialised an eye case which was very infectious. Sister Davis instructed me how to irrigate the eye and to be scrupulous in scrubbing before and after. I looked after him for five days. The Harley Street Surgeon Mr. King, came to see him and was so amazed with his treatment that he went straight to Matron's office and wanted me promoted and given charge of all treatments on the ward. Matron said he demanded that I do my Moorfield Certificate and carry out my duties looking after these patients. But by this time I had made up my mind and I gave in a months notice. Matron said I should apply for my State Enrolled Certificate, and she obtained it for me. She hoped I would return to nursing again.

The job I got in Fords was on machines. I thought the noise during the first few days, would drive me out of my mind. I got bored to tears after a few months. The pay was very good and I had five weeks on days and one week on nights. I took up evening classes and moved to Ilford where I had nice accommodation. I got involved with the local choir in Ilford in 1948. Teresa and I kept up a steady correspondence. I had written to Frances to send me the engagement ring. When she sent it I sold it and bought Lily May a nursing watch instead. Frances had been out with other boys but apparently they did not make the same impression on her, and she asked me to reconsider. I took up English, Typewriting and Advanced Arithmetic. My teachers thought I did very well and advised me to seek a post in the Office in Fords. I tried, but there were no vacancies and the problem was, on account of my age they would have to offer me a higher salary, and they could hire school leavers and give them less, and train them in their own way.

I bought myself a bicycle. After spending two years in Fords in Dagenham, I was transferred to Walthamstow in East London where they required medical staff to cover the first aid department. I went on permanent nights, doing inspection of spare parts for about four hours and then I covered the sick bay. They learned I had been in Moorfields Eye Hospital and I was paid Inspectors money for both, which was higher than first aid sick-bay orderlies were getting. It was a nice job and I was more or less my own boss. I had a lot of trouble with my sinuses and had to go to the Ear, Nose and Throat Hospital nearly every Friday for six months. The infection did not clear up so I had to go into hospital for a "Caldwell Lock", which is a removal of the left antrum as it was full of puss. Professor Ormerod himself did the operation and he drained it: so now if washouts are necessary they are able to insert a plastic tube into the cavity and insert penicillin into it. That was one of the reasons I got a job in the sick bay and many of the ladies employed, used to come to me early so that

Uncle Michael Corkery at hay making

Hay Making in Rossmore

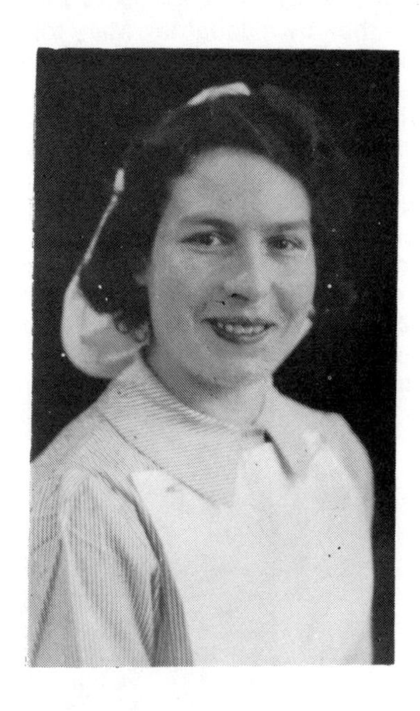

Lily May Nursing in London

they could have treatment there before the Staff Nurse came in. They were not very keen on her for one reason or another. I was drawn towards the nursing profession again. I had nice accommodation with a Polish family; they wanted a Catholic lodger. I kept my bicycle there but could only put on the wireless if they were present. This made me really fed up.

I was looking through the Nursing Mirror one day and saw that there was a sanatorium in Essex which had its own hostel for male nurses. I went down first thing on Monday morning with all my references etc. I met the Matron and she told me I could start. I was the second male nurse to apply so I had a choice of rooms. I chose one with a balcony. The hospital was in a lovely part of the country and had tennis courts, theatre and cinema. I gave in my notice to Fords and told my landlady I was giving her a weeks notice. She was almost in tears, saying the children would miss me and so on. I was glad I had decided to go back Nursing. I felt happier than I had felt for months. I got the position of Staff Nurse and the opportunity to do my Tuberculosis Certificate there. Staff Nurse Kelly was in charge and I was next to her. The money was less than Fords but the work was far more interesting.

During the time I was in Fords in Dagenham, Lily May had been ill with influenza and was very run down after it. The Matron had sent her to Irish friends of ours in Cricklewood — Paddy and Mary Crowley. They had a large boarding house and Mary had known us from our days in Ballygurteen. She stayed there for two weeks where Paddy and Mary looked after her like she was their own daughter. Mary told me that Lily May had met an Irish lad from Killorglin in County Kerry — Owen O'Grady and that they were going out steady together. She had finished her Moorfields training and was thinking of finishing her training at another hospital which the matron was going to get in contact with. When she learned that she was going steady she asked her to bring her young man along to give him the once over. This was the interest she took in all her staff. I was delighted she found someone she loved and after she had been in Rossmore on a holiday on her own, she came back to fix arrangements for the wedding. Fr. John came over to London to marry them on the 11th April, 1950 at Cricklewood. Owen paid for everything. It was a wonderful reception with all Owen's family present. I gave her away and she started her new life in London. But after a few months Owen got a job with the A.A. in Killarney and they settled in Killorglin, where I often spent holidays in later years.

Rossmore Parish Church

CHAPTER VIII

I now had to think of what my future might bring me. Teresa and I were still thinking of settling down, but as I could not get a nursing position in Ireland (except it was mental nursing which I could not compare with general nursing) I settled into Broomfield Hospital very quickly and I got a transfer to the Knights of St. Columba, Council, 302 Chelmsford, and became active with them. I received my second and third degree. This was a great organisation and the brothers in that order are great friends of mine until this very day. I started nursing one week after Lily May's wedding on the 22nd April.

I felt free now to take stock of my own life and do something that would be permanent and lead to a superannuated job with a pension in my old age. With these thoughts in mind it was difficult for Teresa and me to come to grips about her coming to England, but her heart was in Ireland and I could forsee this. There were plenty of nurses who gave me the glad eye and men were scarce so I was told. I found more social life here than when I was in London because you did not have to travel outside the camp. I was very keen on tennis and I played badminton as well. We had a crowd of male nurses, Irish, English, Czechoslavakian. Charge Nurse Jimmy Keane from Tipperary was in charge of the hostel and we became great friends, cinema shows Thursday nights, dances once a fortnight, so there was no time to get bored. There was a big anniversary dance at the Hospital on May 27th, 1950 and I had no partner. I had known the diet cook, who was introduced to me one night when I was leaving the hall. When we were getting short of money or coming near payday we would ring up the cook on night duty and we would steal into the dining hall and ask if she had cooked the night nurses meal yet, and got a free supper. One night I was talking to some of the staff and I asked one of them if she was going to the dance and she said she would if she had a partner. I asked her, and went down to Chelmsford to hire an evening suit. She made her own dress. I knew she was Miss Grove at this stage. She had lovely red hair and dark brown eyes. All the male nurses had dates that night and everyone looked smart. I met her outside the dance hall wearing dickie bow and all the other nurses did likewise. Miss Grove appeared in the distance driven by her father and emerged from the car looking radiant. I took her by the arm and led her to the dance. She was a good dancer, and having met matron and the nurses, we were soon waltzing away to the music. She had a long frock of ribbed taffeta, turquoise in colour and looked very lady like. She could do all the modern English dances and having announced the interval waltz I was on the floor first and we waltzed as if we had been waltzing for years. At the end of that waltz Matron Burnett came over to us and said "Congratulations Mr. Corkery and Miss Grove. You, Miss Grove are the belle of the ball". This expression rang a bell in my memory. When I was in Fords in Dagenham I stayed with an English family. The lady had lost her husband, but her family were in and out to see her. She was good to me, and one night she said she would read my teacup. She told me I would leave Fords and go back to nursing, that I was very discontented there and that I had a gift of healing in my hands if I cared to use it. She told me I was coming to a crossroad in my life and that I didn't know which way to turn. I did not believe her then but I must say that everything she told me came into place. She told me that she saw me at a ball dancing with a lovely girl, and at some part of the evening, someone in authority would approach me and my partner, and she would tell my partner that she was the belle of the ball, and that her initial was E. At that time I did not know Miss Grove's Christian name and I never asked. She told me E was for Elsie. I was told this was the girl I would marry. She was very amused at the time and I felt really happy for the rest of the evening. I took her and her friend Maisie home that night and she was surprised when I kissed her goodnight. We went out steady from then and as the countryside round there was beautiful for walks, we spent a lot of time together. I told her about Teresa and she said I should marry a nice girl like her. To set my conscience free I wrote to Teresa that I found myself falling in love with Elsie. I knew it would be a hard decision for both of us, but as we were separated, and Elsie and I worked together we had a better opportunity of going out together. Elsie was Church of England and was an organist at her own church, and a great supporter of it. We played tennis together and enjoyed each others company. I had an understanding letter from Teresa wishing us both luck. I am deeply grateful for that letter. Now the obstacles really started. Her mother had different ideas for Elsie and encouraged her friendship with a chap named Laurence from the village where Elsie went to church. Elsie suffered most, as she was got at for refusing to give me up, this was the only thing that spoilt our happiness. We went to Benediction together on Sunday evenings in Chelmsford and she was very taken with this ceremony. We used to meet at the wards as she did all the diets etc. Even Miss Wilmot, the assistant matron used to pull our legs about it.

Elsie took me to her church when it was empty and asked my opinion of it. I told her it was a very nice church but one thing was missing. That was the Blessed Sacrament lamp burning in front of the Tabernacle. I explained this to her, and it was like this we went, from step to step explaining the difference between the two Beliefs. I introduced her to Canon WIlson and he gave her a book of questions and answers between a Jesuit priest and Church of England Theologian from Oxford. There were a series of questions that were broadcast on BBC programmes in Australia. She read the book and studied it and thus understood the Catholic teaching better. Her mother threatened to burn it. Difficulties were put in her path from the very beginning. We knew we had a hard road before us and although her Dad got on well with me he never said anything or tried to interfere.

I was taken ill in the Summer of 1950. There was a hospital fete and I was looking after a stall when I got a terrible pain in my left lung. Next day up on the balcony I felt worse and at lunch time I went to Dr. Yells secretary who phoned him to come and see me. He x-rayed me and having screened me he told me to go to bed immediately as I had a shadow on the left lung and that I had Pleurisy. I was put to bed in the hostel and I remember being nursed by the

Matron and Assistant Matron. I was transferred to the ward in a private cubicle and I was there for three long months, bed bathed every other day, Sputum tests and Streptomycin injections etc. and complete bed rest. Dr. Yell was the finest Chest Specialist in that part of England and I'm sure I'd have been dead only for him. All sorts of rumours went out around the hospital. Elsie was cooking the evening meal one evening and one of the nurses said it was a pity that poor Simon had tuberculosis. Poor Elsie dropped everything and went out crying. It was rather tactless that this remark should have been made, and it was breaking the confidentiality between patient and nurse which the other male nurses disapproved of. It was during my stay there, that Elsie applied for a job in London, to get more certificates, although she attained her City & Guilds examinations necessary in catering. She was a beautiful cook and so was her mother. Her mother came to see me one evening at the hospital and asked me to let Elsie choose Laurence, or words to that effect. I said that if Elsie chose to go out with me that was her affair. She told me that she did not like the Irish and that I had been in the war, that I was too old for her, eleven years older. I thanked her for coming to see me and said I would not change my mind. I remember Elsie went to Shanklin on the Isle of Wight on holiday and it was her birthday on the 14th June, I sent her a lovely birthday card and met her at the station. I gave her a lovely compact and when she showed it to her mother, her mother said she should not accept presents from strange men.

I went up to thirteen stone four pounds during my stay in hospital, and flew home to Lily May and spent a fortnights holidays there. During my stay in hospital Elsie wrote nearly every day and she told me in her letters of her search for the truth and of her new interest in the Faith. She walked up and down past St Xaviers Church in Lewisham, and could not make up her mind whether to go in. It was the 8th of December the feast of the Immaculate Conception. When she did go in she said that the crown over Our Lady's statue was all lit up like a jewelled crown and she was very impressed by it. Coincidentally November 1st 1950, the day Elsie moved to London was the day that Pope Pius XII solemnly defined the Corporal Assumption of the Blessed Virgin . I had taught Elsie how to say the Rosary and we often said it together. I suppose our separation at this time of our friendship brought us closer together in that my illness had brought a renewal of Faith into my life, which is what usually happens when we come close to reality.

CHAPTER IX

I was put into the theatre on my return from my Irish holidays and this was new to me as I had done most of my nursing on the wards. I soon lost weight and started perspiring with the heat of the sterilisation units which was my work during the days when we were not operating. Mr. Flavell was the surgeon. He came down from London one day and I was that day, guiding the lamp for him above the table as he was performing a three stage Thoracotomy, and he was explaining the operation to me as he went on. I was so interested in what he was doing that I slipped off the stool and brought the lamp crashing down on his head. Sister Murphy called me all the names under the sun. Another day I was keeping an account of all the gauze swabs which were arranged in packets of five. As they were used they were ticked off on the board for the surgeon to keep his own record so that he could double check before he closed the wound. He had finished the operation and all the swabs had been accounted for except one. He was doing the final closing of the inner layers when we were told there was one missing, so the operation had to come to a standstill. He was a brilliant, accurate, confident and dedicated surgeon. Suddenly I spotted a swab underneath his wellington boot, and to save the disturbing or making things unsterile, I grabbed the long cheedle forceps and reached for the swab. There was an almighty roar. In my eagerness to please, Mr. Flavell and allow him to continue closing the wound, I had caught his toe as well as the swab. The forceps must have really hurt. I apologised and he was very calm saying I was very observant and he was grateful that I had found the swab. Sister Murphy was furious with me but there was a great deal of laughter about it afterwards. Another day, I was guiding the light for Mr. Flavell. Dr. McDaid was the anaesthestist, and he was assisting the operation. He had rather a large head and it got in his Mr. Flavell's light. He shouted 'get your bloody head out of the way McDaid'. I felt sorry for him because I knew how he felt, having been through the mill myself. Another day, Sister Murphy had a date and I was having a shower. She gave me a kick up the behind and almost came under the shower with me, she was in such a hurry. Having worked there, your modesty sometimes made you feel trapped into a society of laughter. Another occasion I remember, was helping a female patient to be bandaged tightly with a "manytailed" bandage. Dr. McDaid was doing this himself, and it was very important that it should help the patient, when he or she coughed during their recovery after the operation. This was very significant in protecting the vibration of coughing and causing slight haemorrage inwardly. I was putting cotton wool on the patient's breasts to give her a feeling of modesty due to my presence in the theatre. Mr. McDaid shouted "For God's sake Corkery, have you never handled a woman's breast before, hold her firm so that the bandage will give her complete support". I thought then that he was a bully, but having watched him come round the wards, all hours of the night, to check on the condition of his patients, I decided he was a very conscientious doctor. I could go on forever describing the funny things that happened on duty. A sense of humour is needed in the nursing profession otherwise one would become very sensitive.

Jack Butler was a man who came to do his Tuberculosis certificate and then on to finish his training. He was a married man who had done shoe-making and lived in South End. He used to cycle home on his days off. He must have found it very hard to live on student's pay. I mentioned what kind of nurse I was. SRN's wore black belts. Those who had other qualifications like preliminary state exams wore red belts. One evening Jack came into the dining hall wearing blue epaulettes with SRBF beautifully done on it. He did not know that the matron was on her rounds and she met him on the corridor. She said "Mr Butler, what does SRBF stand for?". "State Registered Bloody Fool, Matron", he said, and she immediately laughed her head off. I think he got a great ovation when he came into the dining hall. It was there that most of the gossip and happenings were told. Later on I will record my meeting with Jack in the Isle of Wight many years later when our paths cross again. Jack had a droll sense of humour but was a marvellous nurse. John was a student nurse who looked after me when I was a patient. He brought in a Ryles tube to push down into my stomach to obtain some gastric juices. He started off ok. but in doing it, he burnt the whole side of my nose, which was tender after the operation I had had in London and I told him to get out and that he wouldn't make a nurse in a thousand years. What had happened was: there are lead weights in the bottom of the Ryles tube and the side of the tube had burst thus, exposing hot metal. You are taught as a nurse, before you sterilise any equipment you should examine the contents carefully and throw out any faulty equipment or bring it to the notice of the ward sister. A nurse may not always realise that observation is one of the leading qualities in the prospective student nurse, because this is one quality that makes the practical nurse far above those who may be good in theory, but cannot put it into practice.

We had a private bus for going down into Chelmsford. It went there three times a day, at 9 a.m., 2 p.m., and at 6 p.m. Staff, coming and going had this facility. It was also useful for taking us to Mass on Sundays. Mass was in a private house which was taken over by the council. It had a private chapel with a confessional. A priest from Chelmsford came out to say Mass. One Sunday morning some people were waiting for Confession and the priest was late and there was only standing room. I slipped into the Confessional with my raincoat over my uniform. One of the lads told Noreen Nyland to to go Confession and the poor girl started off the usual prayers. I thought it had gone far enough at this stage and told her to say the Rosary as a penance. She was very embarrassed and going back on the bus everyone was laughing about it. In the meantime she had borrowed a hat pin from Nurse McCloud and put it in the sole of her shoe. She then gave me a kick through the seat, driving the hat pin into my behind with a vengeance. I gave a scream and she said "That will be your penance". Noreen Nyland went on to finish her training in Romford General Hospital. If this book is ever published I hope it will bring back happy memories. Noreen, I hope God has forgiven me, but you know I was always a trickster without counting the consequences. I remember well, Ted Cooper who later on married Maisie Burns, Nurse McCloud, Derek Spence, Staff Nurse Kelly, Michael Van Damm, Jimmy Duffield, Jimmy Keane and many others. I know where some of them went but I would like to know where the rest are. Mr. McManus who was an old timer at Broomfield Hospital has now got a Papal Decoration for his work in the Church in Chelmsford. I have through Mac, kept in touch and also with Canon Manning, now Parish Priest of the parish, who many years previously gave me his blessing as a newly ordained priest in the yard in Derrymore Longford. A great pillar of the church was Canon Wilson, later Monsignor Wilson, who did so much for Elsie and me during the years that followed.

Essex County Hospital, Broomfield, Chelmsford

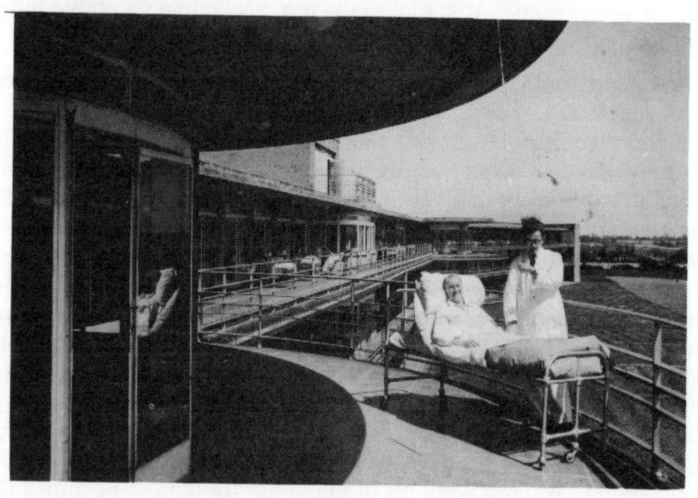

Male Nurse Keane from Tipperary on Balcony Broomfield Hospital

CHAPTER X

I think I had at this time put Laurence off Elsie's trail, and we started going to shows in London. We went to see Carousel on the 26th January 1951 and had a lovely evening. We caught the last train home from Liverpool Street Station and it only went as far as Shenfield. We had to hire a taxi from there to Elsie's home in Broomfield. I remember how happy we were. She loved the shows as much as I did. We had been to several other shows before this, which were organised by the Hospital Social Club. We went to see Tom Arnolds show Rose Marie on ice. Barbara Anne Scott was the leading lady. That was one of the nicest shows I ever saw. Michael Kirby was the leading man. They both came from Canada. Michael Kirby danced with Sonia Henie, the great Hollywood film star, who made so many lovely films on ice. We went to see Annie Get Your Gun in South End, which was another great performance. I applied for a position in Brook General Hospital in London which was at the time the greatest fever hospital in London. Fever Hospitals had lost their use and had only a few wards, a Thoracic Unit and a Neuro Surgical unit opened newly. Some of the leading surgeons were in our unit. Mr. Clancy, Mr. McArthur and Mr. Whitehead and also another person whose name I cannot recall.

I was accepted by Matron Monaghan who was the Irish Matron, and having worked a months notice I said goodbye to all the staff at Broomfield and Miss Wilmot, who wished me every luck. This was the hospital that was the forming of my interest in my vocation of nursing and which was only a start in the years that lay ahead.

My sister Molly had married Noel McGeeney. Owens brother Paul got married on April 11th, my birthday and Lily May's Wedding Anniversary. My father had left Loughill National School and went to teach at Stone Park National School. About the time of my birthday, Elsie and I cycled to Pleshey and went to a dance there in the evening. I had also taken her to see a football match at Mitcham, between Mayo and Meath. I was gradually introducing her to Irish games, as if climatising her to the Irish way of life. We attended the wedding reception of Paul O'Grady and his bride Mary Madden, a girl from Limerick at Nellies Home in London. I also took Elsie to a hurling match between Tipperary and Galway.

I started work on the Thoracic Unit on May 16th, 1951 and I met the ward sister, Sister Hynes. She was very strict but just, and she was a real professional. I learned a lot from her and I was the only male nurse on the unit who was permanent. The Female and Male Nurse Staff Nurses did a six months course here to obtain their Thoracic certificate and also next door at the Neurosurgical Unit for a further six months to gain another certificate there. Sister Hynes taught me more than any ward sister has ever taught me and being Irish herself, I had no difficulty in forming a great friendship with her. When it came to off duty, she gave me any evening I wanted, or helped me in any way she could. It was nice for me to be in London near Elsie. She had applied for a position at the Middlesex Hospital and got a position as second in command, she was studying for a diploma in Hygiene. I was able to entertain her to tea, with our own sitting room, and television. This was a great saving, because of the expense of food. I had a nice room to myself overlooking the tennis courts. The hospital was situated in a lovely spot, half-way between Blackheath and Woolwich. The Army Military Hospital was next door called the Hibbert Hospital and if we were on Sunday duty we went to Mass there. I used to get a Green Line bus up to London to see Elsie and I often had to rush to catch the last coach leaving Victoria. We really loved London at this time. It was recovering again after the war and the night life was fantastic. Things were easier for me now that I was away from Essex, and although Elsie's mother did not wholeheartedly approve I'm sure she was coming round. She threatened she would not come to the wedding if it came to one. Elsie was rushed into hospital with appendicitis on June 7th 1951 and was operated on that night. I went to see her every day and took her roses and carnations. I had applied to the RAF for some money that was due to people who took up employment in the Civil Service and had been members of the forces for so many years. It was through another male nurse that I heard about it and he told me where to apply. I got about one hundred pounds. It was a great surprise. I had intended getting engaged to Elsie on her 21st birthday 14th June 1951 but we postponed the date because of her going into hospital. We chose a ring in a little jewellers shop in the High Street, Catford. It was second hand and the jeweller fully recommended it. There was so much purchase tax on the rings, we were told we would not get the value of the ring. It was a neat engagement ring, with three white diamonds. The size was altered so it would fit properly. It was eighteen carat gold. We went for a drink and Elsie requested to go to the Catholic Church in Lewisham, where she had seen the statue of Our Lady, St. Xavier's Church. Having said a prayer in front of the Sacred Heart altar, she accepted the ring on her finger and since that day we both have a special devotion to the Sacred Heart, it being the month of the Sacred Heart as well. I went back on duty that evening and received the congratulations of all the nurses. Now at last our prayers were heard. Thank God. We were progressing slowly towards the great day.

I went for a holiday to Lily May's and Owen's, I think it was about February. Patrick was born and about six months old at this stage. I helped Lily May but Owen saw me pushing the pram along the road from Killorglin to Killarney and he became mad about it. Irishmen did not push prams in public in those days apparently. I had a lovely holiday and I went to see all the O'Grady family, who were always so good to me, and are to this day. Meanwhile, in London Elsie was busy with her evening classes. I wrote to her often and Lily May and Owen were delighted we were engaged. I had several letters from her and I had one letter which said she would like me to return on Sunday morning instead of Monday. I know I said to Lily May "I wonder if anything is wrong". Lily May said, "She is now a Catholic I'm sure and she took advantage of the fact that you were out of the country to do so, and she wants you to go to Holy Communion with her on Sunday morning". I flew back to London and before we went to Mass she said she wanted me to come up to the altar with her as she was making her First Holy Communion in the Catholic Church, at the back of the Middlesex Hospital. Thus, she could say she was received without any pressure from me. It was Fr. McLaughlin who instructed Elsie. He was a friend of Fr. Johns. It was at a dance in Lewisham when we were walking up the hall and Elsie said there is the priest I saw in the dream one evening when I passed out after finishing work at 6 p.m. She said she still does not understand what happened to her, but she walked straight up to this priest and told him she had seen him before, and that she had been praying at the time about becoming a Catholic. That was a coincidence that she has not solved. Our Lady must have been looking after her during all this time and her great devotion to Our Lady has been fantastic during all these years, and hopefully, please God, it will continue. Elsie went home for a week-end after we had got engaged, but her mother did not show much interest although she did attend a party for her 21st birthday. Her dad seemed pleased and wished her every happiness. Meantime, Elsie had in the course of her duties prepared meals for Lord Montgomery and Lady Astor.

Elsie and me at the Festival of Britain 1951

E

CHAPTER XI

It was in 1952, that Kathleen and four other nuns arrived in London, on their way to Belgium to the Mother House, where they were to have their final profession. I took a taxi surrounded by five nuns from Euston Station to Westminister Cathedral for morning Mass. I was delighted to see Kathleen after all these years, and her friends were really happy to be coming over, and they were ali looking forward to making their final profession. They were all chattering to me, and some of the people round Westminister Cathedral must have wondered what someone like me was doing surrounded by so many nuns, because it was rare during those years, for young nuns, to be accompanied by some male like myself in his early thirties.

Another great event in London in 1952 was Fr. Peyton's Rosary Crusade in Wembly Stadium, Elsie and myself were present there, and the huge crowd that came from all over London and from the provinces, was a living testament of the devotion this Irish Priest had for the Rosary all his life, he was the Priest that was miracously cured of Tuberculosis, as he promised 1 million souls to Our Lady if she could cure him and help him become a Priest. There were 90,000 at this rally, and again all the marshalling was done by the Knights of St. Columba on Sunday, 27th July, 1952 at 3 p.m. The Drama groups depicted the Mysteries of the Rosary and brought hope to the huge audience. The Joyful Mysteries were demonstrated by the Catholic Stage Guild, Challaner Club Dramatic Society, the Grail, St. Andrews Dramatic Society, Streatham St. Anns Dramatic Society, Vauxhall, St. Anthony's Players, Sutton; St. Clement Players, Ewell.

Sorrowful Mysteries: The Companions of the Cross in association with Brockley Catholic Dramatic Club, Catholic Police Guild Dramatic Society; Guildhall players, Ilford; St. Margarets Dramatic Society, Camden Town; St. Nicholas Players, Manor Park; Upminister Dramatic Club.

The Glorious Mysteries were portrayed by nine other groups from Kent, Sidcup, Catford, Romford in Essex. This display of Faith and devotion to Mary, was one of the best organised Crusades in England. Most of the vast crowd signed The Family Rosary Crusade. Fr. Patrick Peyton had worked on this idea from 1948 as a young Priest, his great saying then and has been ever since is that, 'The Family that prays together, stays together'. Crusades were organised in London, Ontario, United States, Alaska.

The Rally at Wembley Stadium that began on 27th July 1952, became worldwide and in 1953 moved on to Newfoundland. The Arch Diocese of New York and the Family Rosary Apostle as he was known moved on to Australia, South America and the Philippines, he also covered Spain, and even up to the present time, you can hear him speak on the Family Rosary in America and Ireland on his return visit, he was a young Priest in 1948 and now years later he still talks, and spreads the devotion. Surely his souls brought closer to God through the Rosary and Our 'Lady must surely run into millions. Elsie was very impressed by him and for someone new to the Catholic Faith, it was the zeal of thought and devotion that we witnessed that day that has left its mark to this day, Thank God.

We planned away for our wedding and I obtained a flat near Woolwich where I lived for many weeks, but I was taken ill, and later on when I was nursing a tuberculosis patient in the ward one night he told me of a flat that would be unfurnished and very reasonable rent, and it did become available about three weeks before the wedding. This was great news for both of us, and we started getting bits and pieces together, although in the furnished flat I had rented, I lost some lovely sheets, we had received as a wedding present from Elsie's mother.

We went to a wedding of Jean and Ernie in Chelmsford in Essex in January 1953. We were great friends of theirs, and they often come to Ireland to see us, and have spent happy holidays at our house in the Isle of Wight, when we were in Shanklin.

The day was now set for our wedding, April 11th 1953, I wrote to my old friend, Charge Nurse Keane in Broomfield, but he said he could not be my best man as he was emigrating to Canada. So, I had a male nurse who worked with me in the Brook hospital, Ron King, Elsie and I were good friends of his and another nurse at the Brook hospital, Esther Donnelly, who was bridesmaid, so as the day approached we had already asked Fr. John to come over from Ireland to perform the ceremony. We had the flat all furnished out and had arranged for our honeymoon in Ireland, all the air tickets bought and Elsie's parents had hired a hall in Broomfield and got a catering firm to do the breakfast or lunch as you might call it. Fr John came over a couple of weeks before the wedding and stayed at our flat, and then the great day came. I arranged for a fortnights holiday and we travelled down to Broomfield the day before. I was so excited that I got out at the wrong station and brought Fr. John out on the platform with me, it was Fr. John who noticed we got out at the wrong station. Elsie's mother had a very busy time putting guests up for the wedding. The best man Ron King and myself, stayed with a first cousin of Elsie's and Fr. John stayed in a hotel beside the Church. Fr. John was playing the piano and enjoying a glass of beer and really made himself at home, so much that Elsie's mother took a great liking to him and I think it was Fr. John's easy manner that made her look on Catholics in a new light, and they have been great friends over the years and he holds her in great respect. Elsie's mother put up my Aunt Maud, Esther Donnelly, Nellie Riordan and Joan. I don't know how she managed to put them all up. We hired two cars and a coach to bring the guests and bridesmaids and best man to the Church. Elsie and Fr. John were driving about collecting the flowers etc. Ron and I went up to Broomfield for a short while and we had a quiet drink, but it was a very quiet stag party if you could call it that. We went down to see Canon Wilson to go to confession but we were too late, so had to go down early next morning. The wedding was arranged for 10 a.m. the next morning in the Church of the Immaculate Conception in

The Corkery Family in Longford on the day of our visit

Chelmsford, the Church we both attended Benediction in, on earlier years in Broomfield hospital.

The great morning had arrived and Ron and I in our best suits walked to the Church about half an hour before the ceremony should start, as we both wanted to go to confession. Canon Wilson was nowhere around and Fr. John was not allowed to hear my confession, so I was getting into a state of panic at this time, anyhow he arrived with all the guests and Elsie had already arrived, and she was told to wait outside as I was not at the altar. She was getting really worried and thought I had taken myself away, and that I was not going through with it. But then as Canon Wilson had given me his little lecture on the new vocation in my life, and preparing myself for it, he let me go and I will say that there was a sigh of relief when I took up my position at the altar. Fr. John was there ready to start the ceremony. Cecil Gladwell, one of the Knights of Columba and a great friend of mine played the wedding march and Elsie was allowed to enter with her Father, Esther Donnelly and Maisie Bohannan as bridesmaids, and Joan Riordan, Elsie's sister Audrey and two page boys, twin boys Simon and Paul Jackson, and Nellie Riordan.

The following report appeared in the local press, under the heading: "The Bride made the Dresses".

'The wedding was solemnised at the Church of the Immaculate Conception, Chelmsford on Saturday of Miss Elsie Lorna Grove, elder daughter of Mr and Mrs F. S. Grove of the Warren Jubilee Avenue, Broomfield with Mr James Simon Corkery, second son of Mr P. J. O'Brien Corkery N.T., of Stonepark, Longford, Eire. The Rev. J. P. Corkery, brother of the bridegroom officiated.

The bride given away by her father, wore white figured satin Queen Anne style dress with train and headdress of orange blossom, and she carried pink carnations, fresias and trailing fern.

The bridemaids were the Misses Esther Donnelly, Maisie Bohannan, Audrey Grove sister, and Joan O'Riordan. Esther and Maisie wore pink taffeta trimmed with blue and carried blue irises, pink tulips and fresias; Joan and Audrey wore blue taffeta trimmed with pink, and carried posies of mixed spring flowers. Their blue pendant necklaces, and gold bracelets were gifts of the bridegroom. Masters Paul and Simon Jackson twin cousins of the bride, were page boys in white blouses, and long blue trousers and ties, they received tie pins from the bridegroom. Mr. R. King was best man.

Mr. Gladwell was at the organ for Nuptial Mass and the Papal Blessing was received. The bride's parents gave a reception at the Church Hall Broomfield for 50 guests.

The many gifts included cutlery from the brides fellow workers at the Middlesex Hospital and a clock from the bridegrooms colleagues at the Brook General Hospital, Woolwich.

For the honeymoon by air to Ireland the bride travelled in a green "bird's-eye-check" costume with brown accessories.

The bride made her own dress and also those of her four bridesmaids.'

Our honeymoon first in Dublin, where we spent the first night in a hotel which is no longer there, was a peaceful happy memory. Of course we did discover that a few of our friends had after all got to our suitcases, and as we emptied the bag, confetti covered the floor of the bedroom and pyjamas were sewn up in some bizarre fashion. Thank God for the other presents of pyjamas. What with doors banging and dripping taps and a huge jar hot water bottle rolling out of bed, it was more like an obstacle race. The knock on the door next morning with the cup of tea found me in the middle of the floor with Elsie's hairbrush brushing up the confetti much to the laughter of the cailin that brought the tea. After a beautiful cooked breakfast, we made our way to Mass in the nearest Church to Parnell Square.

We continued our walk around Dublin and made discreet inquiries about our journey to Longford to meet our side of the family. A friendly policeman told us that we were too late for a bus, so he bargained with a taxi-driver to take us there and back for £7.00. We stopped at Mullingar and had lunch, and from there I phoned Daddy to tell him we were on our way and he said he would like to speak to Elsie. Poor Elsie looked aghast when I told her, because she did not have the pleasure of meeting him as yet. After a few seconds talking to Daddy, she seemed very relieved and seemed thrilled as Daddy was always an expert in communicating, I suppose his years of experience as a teacher would have given him that gift. At least she had broken the ice, and we arrived there on Sunday afternoon to meet the whole family who were all lined up outside the gate to welcome us, all eleven of the children. I don't suppose Elsie will ever forget that moment, and Baby's sister Molly and her husband were there to meet us also. Molly was a great friend of mine from my first arrival in Derrymore from West Cork, and still is to this very day. We had a wonderful home coming and they all liked Elsie and they said then, as they have repeated on many occasions since, that Elsie's entrance to the Corkerys was the best thing that ever happened to them. I am sure Daddy was very pleased that at last his Prodigal son had settled, and that a loving, shy and charming girl had brought happiness to his life.

We travelled back to Dublin and arrived back to find Father John who had flown back from London, and who had decided to stay at the hotel for that night, we were brought up to date with the rest of the news regarding my Aunty Maud, and who he told us had planned to fly over with us until he restrained her. We had a great evening with him and next day he took us both out to dinner to a restaurant called 'The Green Rooster'. A funny thing happened when I was hanging up my coat and scarf leaving John and Elsie sitting at the table as John was well known there, as the waitress saw me approaching from the end of the room, she stopped and looked at me as if she was in a state of shock, until she looked back at the table to see if Fr. John was there. It was then she realised we were brothers and that Fr. John had got his clerical collar so I was relieved and on many occasions since then on my travels throughout Ireland, I have been asked if I was indeed Fr. Corkery's brother, so

Miss Taylor who took us round the Ring of Kerry

The Wishing Stone Blarney Castle

Kissing the Blarney Stone

I have to watch my P's and Q's as there is only eleven months between us and the resemblance must be very close.

We travelled down to Kerry to meet Lily May and Owen with whom we were going to stay in Killorglin. Elsie enjoyed the train journey and the lovely scenery, and we were given a warm welcome, and we spent nearly ten days in Kerry altogether. We were wined and dined at the O'Grady household and by Miss Taylor who took us round the Ring of Kerry and Killarney and such was our inner happiness over long walks in Killorglin, the hospitality of all the Killorglin people, we were taken to Blarney Castle which was indeed a beautiful memory. It was sad to leave Killorglin, we had a honeymoon which has lasted in our memories till this day now 36 years hence.

We were taken to Rossmore in West Cork and met by my Uncle Michael and Muriel and his daughter Josephine, we were given a great welcome, and we saw the village where he taught and his land that surrounded the village, so she had now seen all the happy places which were connected with my younger days.

Having travelled back to Dublin we went to one of the shows and next day we went out to Maynooth to meet Fr. John who gave us a conducted tour of Maynooth, he was Librarian there for twenty five years, this was the "Tostal" period in Ireland, and he showed us round the museum and the different things he had contributed himself, during his years as Librarian. I do not want to go into detail in this Autobiography concerning Fr. John because he has made his mark on the culture scene in Ireland as successor to Fr. Hayes in Muintir na Tire for years. His reviews on the book scene review on Sunday evening on R.T.E. Radio with Anthony O'Mahony, his four years as head of the Abak College in Nigeria and his many other accomplishments in the Field of Learning as I am sure someone somewhere will do him the credit he deserves, not only here but in America. I can only pay tribute to him in a small way, but wherever I have travelled in England and Ireland, people have come forward and paid him glowing tributes, yet he retains that humility that has been the quality that Daddy personified in his teaching ability which held him in high esteem not only in Longford but throughout the world. In Australia, New Zealand, America and foreign lands he gave them the opportunity when references were needed from him. I could go on about his private teaching at home in the house in Derrymore where poor pupils who could not afford the books and the private tuition which he gave freely, especially to the less fortunate.

We were sad leaving Dublin Airport and Elsie did not want to return, she was so taken up with the people of Ireland, and to our surprise we were approached by a reporter at Dublin, who asked us if we had enjoyed Ireland, and when he heard that we had been on our honeymoon, we were told we were to be the guests of the B.B.C. "In town tonight" and we were told again on our flight over, we would be met at the airport and taken to dinner at some well known restaurant. Everyone on the plane was congratulating us and I had informed Daddy by telephone that he should listen in. As we got off the aircraft

Fr. John

Fr. John Abak College Nigeria

in Heathrow, we were informed that the B.B.C. Radio car had broken down and that they were taking another couple on the next flight in. Naturally, it was a great disappointment but maybe if God spares me for our Golden Jubilee, perhaps we might do the return trip in a different set up. Anyhow, we arrived at our flat in London and pushed shilling after shilling into the electricity metre as we were in complete darkness. At last after so many coins being pushed in, it came on.

We settled down to married life together, happy but slightly disappointed, at what could have been a great finale to our honeymoon. Back to work for both of us, myself to the Brook General Hospital where I got a great welcome from patients and staff who of course asked if I had kissed the Blarney Stone. Elsie back to the Middlesex hospital to continue in her catering career. In October of 1953, we were both taken ill vomiting and there was no one even to help us, as the people above us were busy because her husband was not so well, we think it was the lead in the paint decorating the flat that did it. Anyhow I almost crawled out to a little shop down the road and got some Bovril which saved us and the vomiting stopped. We had realised that Elsie was expecting and finding it difficult to get about. Elsie's Mum and Dad visited us at Christmas and they told us they were trying to secure a house for us in Essex near their home. Elsie packed up work at this stage and we started preparing for a job in St. John's hospital in Chelmsford. Elsie arranged travel down to her own home in Broomfield just three miles from Chelmsford. I succeeded in getting a nursing position at St. John's Hospital but I had to work a month's notice.

Elsie was rushed into hospital in Woolwich in London and John our son was born on January 4th 1954. As I was giving her the news that we had got a house over the phone the Ward Sister informed me that I had a baby son. So that I will always remember January 4th 1954 as a very happy day for both of us. New Job, New House and New Baby, what a great start to our marriage, we were now a family unit "Deo Gratias". So it was in 77 Beehive Lane, Chelmsford that a whole new life was before us as we owe a debt of gratitude to Elsie's parents for their generosity and consideration.

Elsie and myself with two of our children

Our first worry about our son John was his rash which was diagnosed as Eczema and later chest complaints, we were told that he had Asthma. When one was bad the other complaint improved, we were not allowed to wash him with water, he had to have warm olive oil applied to his whole body, cleaned off gently with a soft towel. He was scratching and shaking his cot although he was wrapped up in gauze and bandages until tubular gauze came on the market, the only ointment available at this time was a yellow sulphur ointment. It was an hours work each evening before putting him down for the night. Elsie had many a sleepless night and it got her down at times, as she tried to save me from getting wakened up so that I at least would be able to concentrate on my nursing career.

I thought that she would be turned off having any more children, but Angela my daughter was born on the 2nd May 1955, it was a beautiful after-

Elsie very happy with two of our children

noon at St. John's Hospital and we had a phone call to the ward telling me to come home as soon as possible. As I was cycling home, the ambulance passed me on the way and I arrived home too late, so I made some tea and had something to eat. I started walking up and down the garden and towards nine o'clock I decided to ring up and of course it was all over a few hours, so I cycled in to the Maternity Ward. Miss Murphy the mid-wifery Superintendant met me on the corridor and she said you have a lovely red haired daughter with so much hair she looks like a lavatory brush. Elsie was disgusted with me, as she had been waiting since 7 p.m. but we were very happy on this occasion. She was delighted it was a girl and we agreed to call her Angela Maria after my favourite sister, Angela Corkery, Maria after her grandmother and also being the month of Our Lady. I took Elsie in a beautiful nightdress, pale green seersucker trimmed with a broderie anglaise and I felt so proud of her. All the nurses were admiring it, and I took it home to wash a couple of days later, and boiled it with the sheets and when I brought it out and dried it, I had a white nightie and green sheets. When I produced it at the hospital again she cried her heart out and I really felt mad about it. Nanny who was looking after John was disgusted and said one of her favourite Essex expressions "Well, I never". She was doing John's dressings and I was holding him on the kitchen table. Nanny kept repeating "Poor little old boy, it is a shame", meaning his rash. The incident about the nightie went round the hospital and there was a great laugh about Corkery's wife's nightie, the price of popularity does not pay off.

Elsie returned home soon after and we settled down to married life again, she was delighted with Angela as she was the easiest of our children to rear and she was my pride and joy, it took away from the hard nights Elsie had had with John although it wasn't his fault. All went smoothly until the next calamity which was when we put the two in the pram together and the pram got broken.

Canon Wilson "Lord have mercy on him", who came every Thursday without fail to give Holy Communion to all mothers of small children in the Parish, gave Elsie so many words of comfort in the days when John's rash was really bad. She used to say to him but Father I am able to walk to Church on Sunday. "I still want to give you Holy Communion", such dedication of Parish work. He was also Chaplain to the Prison, and his visits to the hospital, and the sick, and the joy he brought to the kids in the children's ward, when he would carry a huge bag of sweets for them and it did not matter to him, what denomination they were, all were welcome to meet him. I have known many Priests in my years in England and I found out their dedication was first class, but he gave so much joy to all. He called a spade a spade in his homily from the pulpit, and he preached a wonderful sermon on the love and mercy of God, but he expected no half measures, he was gentle, firm and kind, and he was responsible for a great number of converts to the faith. It was Canon Wilson who gave the leading light to Elsie when she first approached him. He christened three of our children. Eileen was born twelve months after Angela on the 7th May

1956. Eileen was born at home but the district nurse had a long wait for her. I again arranged my holiday to coincide with her birth and I was waiting around all night, daylight came through the bedroom window, it was a glorious morning, birds were singing and I laid down on the bed and left the district nurse beside Elsie waiting for the big moment and they were to be awakened by me with a cup of tea. Apparently I fell fast asleep and Eileen stole her way into this harsh world, but I slept till it was all over. The birds sang and sang and I felt thrilled to have another girl now three in family. My first words on seeing her "sure she looks like a real Irish colleen" and I chose the name Eileen, she was like a song in my heart. I even took her to the church the same Sunday, Elsie's brother with me and Canon Wilson had chosen a great friend of his Mrs Wilson who was her godmother and another gentleman named Maguire. Nanny had done some cooking and we had a quiet but nice little party back at 77 Beehive Lane.

Now we had our hands full, but with Elsie's talents at making clothes, designing vests and tubular gauze sleeves for dressings for John that the Consultant at the hospital called the Nurses and Sisters and showed what a housewife could do in saving dressings in the case of skin disease. She was also approached by the Consultant at the post-natal clinic and asked "Well, Mrs Corkery what is your advice to these ladies for getting back your figure after your babies and your waist line is I believe 23 ins? she did nothing more than to say "Hard Work".

We bought a twin pram for taking the children to Mass on Sunday. We usually went to a Mass centre which had been opened in the nearby village. It was a village hall made of corrugated iron. It was not very large, and there was a billiard table in the centre of the hall with chairs arranged around it. The altar had to be erected each Sunday and was on trestles. Some foreign Priests provided the Mass and one of these was rather short and plump. One Sunday, he went to turn round, and his fat tummy sent the Altar and everything on it flying, causing much holding of breath and an awesome hush but all was soon put in order and the accident was fortunately not repeated on any other occasion.

We had been to Ireland on holiday in between times, and we stayed with Lily May and Owen in Killorglin, she had now moved to a larger house where she had a few hens. She was feeding them one afternoon when she was picked by a grey hen on a mole in her right leg. I had phoned the doctor, who came to see her and she was rather worried about it, and dressed it for her, and she had to rest her leg for a few days. Elsie helped out and was able to look after Patrick and take some of the work-load off her but we had to return to England. Little did we know at that time that things for Lily May would become so serious even fatal as she had to go and see a Specialist as a lump had come up in her groin, as a result of her leg. Lily May gave birth to a baby girl and they had now moved to Dublin.

On April 5th, 1957 I was rushed to hospital in St. John's with stomach ulcers, at first I was taken to the Surgical ward and they were going to operate on me. The Australian Surgeon, Mr. Muir thought I was too young to operate on, so I was transferred to the medical ward next door for a course of medical treatment and I was put under the care of the Medical Consultant Dr. Sleigh Johnston, who ordered a milk drip for me immediately. I was still vomiting dark brown fluid which is known in the medical profession as Coffee grounds. Fr. John and Philomena flew over from Ireland to see me as I was pretty rough at this time. They put a tube down my stomach, but I put it down myself as I was able to tolerate it better that way. After about thirtysix hours I found it hard to tolerate it, so the doctor told me to take it out and I had to take 2 ozs of milk hourly, I must have been there about six weeks in all. When I came back on duty again I was put on that ward again where Sister Logan kept me under her wing and the nursing care I was given was superb. I was allowed milk and two biscuits in between meals. I responded well to treatment and I had meals arranged in the hospital dining room when I had chicken for lunch every day. One day, the matron came round and found me having a drink of milk on the ward and I was in deep trouble and she said I would have to bring in my pint of milk and have it with my lunch. Sister Logan tried to put in a good word for me and I was having severe pains at times as the work was heavy enough going and I had to be readmitted for treatment. Dr. Sleigh-Johnston looked after me very well and came to see me on the ward and asked me if I was sticking to my diet and I told him yes but that I was not able to get my milk hourly. I should not have said anything, but he met the matron on the corridor and challenged her about the milk and he said if one of your nurses refused to give a patient on the ward his two hourly feed, what would you say to her? and Mr. Corkery is of your own staff and you treat him like this or words to that effect. When she came round the ward after that, I was really scared of her and went to the toilet until she went to the next ward. She was polite to me, but her manner was strict and by the book. She was one of the Old School who believed that nurses should carry on come what may. Thank God for my wife who had prepared diets for me, egg custards, chicken and fish diets and she did that for ten years. She is still doing it so when we ever go out to a Social evening and chicken is on the menu "not again" and I try to get something else to replace it. Life went on, and on July 25th 1958 our third daughter Elizabeth was born.

I tried to get into the Prison Service as the money in nursing was so poor, that it was a financial worry. I was having tablets to relieve the pain, and of course with Bronchitis as well. Anyhow I was called for interview and went before the medical officer, and I think my own Doctor Dr. Stone must have phoned him up, and he said something about my ulcer, so I was turned down because of the danger of one blow from any of the inmates to the stomach and the nature of the work was so vastly different, that my heart would overule my head. So I suppose it was good advice, but the money worries continued for us, we were getting paid monthly and we were now buying the house at this time. I think it was about £28 — £30 a month to feed a wife myself and four children.

I took up part time work on my half day and day off, and I had at this time acquired a tandem and I got a Watsonian side car that would take ladders so myself and another English chap started cleaning windows, he would do the tops and I would do the bottom windows, that was great, but he was taking all the wages. I got the contracts and I got the contract of a large house 365 windows I believe. He was in debt so my wife was giving him his dinner, and also elevenses every morning, so we parted as I was not gaining out of it financially.

I started out painting the interior of the Odeon Cinema and the manager was very nice. I told him what I was doing and he felt sorry for me and I was making a good job of it; one afternoon having painted the inside, facing the public coming in, in the afternoon I spotted the midwifery Supertintendant Miss Murphy. As a nurse you are not allowed to work for anybody else, and especially as I was not on the matrons good books, I turned my back when Miss Murphy was coming up the steps and one eye on her, and trying to paint the windows, the manager came over, he said "do you realise you have painted two panes of glass white". When he realised why I did it, he was laughing his head off and I finished it that week, I got £21 for doing it and I was thrilled.

I also had an ordinary cycle with a cyclemaster wheel in the back and I travelled down to Chatham one day to see my Aunt Maud and I did it all in the one day. I used to travel to Southend on it as well, and it was an easy way of travel. Now that we had four children. Elizabeth was quite a baby and as we could not afford a car I got a seat in front of me to put John on, on the cross-bar of the tandem; where Elsie's handle-bars were, Angela sat in her own little chair. Eileen behind Elsie on the carrier with a chair on that, and Elizabeth in the Watsonian side-car, we went down to the Parish Church in London road, Chelmsford on Sundays. I remember one Sunday after Mass, we were all on it coming home when a man selling papers in the High Street stopped and saw us, he shouted across the street "You should be in the "News of the World," I have seen everything now, six people on a tandem". I think the whole street was looking at us by now. These are the memories we cherish when we compare the present with the past, we had so much joy from that one tandem, and the kids enjoyed it. We had our sorrows and our joys side by side.

One evening there was a bus strike and one of the ward maids, an Irish girl wanted a lift down the town so I took her on the tandem behind me, she got the idea of working the pedals all right, and we gathered up speed and I had gone about 200 yards when she sharted shouting "I have lost my shoe", so we had to go back and pick up the shoe. Another time Elsie started getting ready to go out to the pictures, and I said "Lets get a babysitter" so we asked the girl next door to look after the children, so off we went on the tandem to the cinema, and we were really enjoying it, it was the first time we had been out alone from the children and we called in to the Long Bar and had a coffee and some cakes, all the Teddy boys and girls were hanging round the door so we went for a cycle round the park as if we had not a care in the world, it was so nice to be alone for a few hours at least. Another time I had a half day off, and it was a lovely day and as Elsie's sister Audrey was a frequent visitor at our house Elsie said to me why don't you take Audrey out on the tandem, and off we went to Southend for the afternoon, I cannot remember whether we had a swim or not but I think I had, and we had some tea and cycled home again; it was quite a run from Chelmsford, I said to Elsie when I got home, "do you know I am more tired with Audrey on the back that when you are behind me". And Audrey burst out laughing and she told me then, that she put her feet up going and coming back. No wonder I was tired.

I must include some anecdotes concerning my stay at St. John's Hospital. One Sunday afternoon I was giving out the teas in the Ward during visiting hours. I was filling out the tea into the cups with the large teapot, and one of the patients said "You're Elsie's husband I believe" "Yes, I am" "Well I knew Elsie before you met her, she plays the organ, and you have a very talented wife" "Oh yes" I said "I realise that, but there was one silly old devil who tried to court her, a fellow by the name of Laurence, but I beat him to it". He burst out laughing and says "He happens to be my brother" The teapot in my hand started shaking, and I was pouring it everywhere except into the cups there was a great laugh round the ward as all the visitors were listening to our conversation. Tea was over and a female doctor came in to see this same patient, Erythema Nodosa was the skin disease he had, which he got from attending animals. I had given out the medicines and was at the next bed, when she was going through his past history, she was sitting very close to him taking notes very seriously in her questions, as doctors do, in trying to form a diagnosis. Suddenly, she said to him "And what is your occupation". "I am a Certified Inseminator". She moved her position quickly to the end of the bed blushing as she went, and then he included two words "of Cattle" and they both saw the funny side of it by now, so that everyone of his pals were laughing also.

On another occasion we had a fancy dress ball at the hospital and all the nurses were looking forward to it, it was the conversation for weeks. I came out with an idea that I would dress up as Laika because it was round the time that the Russians had launched a dog in Space, so Elsie fixed me up in a white suit zipped up front, and I had got a face mask, I had an alarm clock inside and a lighted torch shining through the suit. Anyhow, one of the consultant surgeons was adjudicating and I was awarded second prize for the most original one of the evening. All the nurses were dancing around with me after the award, and they tried to get me in to conversation, but I kept on barking from time to time, they even lifted up my trouser leg to see if they could recognise me, and then one of the nurses felt my hand she says "I know who it is, lovely soft hands, they're Corkery's hands, a male nurse's hands. They were at their wits end trying to find out, but it was only at the end of the evening after dancing with me as I had removed my gloves which were attached to the suit. Elsie had designed the suit out of an old sheet. I had two nice hair brushes in a leather case as my award. I still have got these brushes although God knows, there is little hair to brush now.

Another time, I was on the Geriatric Ward at Christmas and each ward was decorated in some theme or another, we adopted a Chinese scene for our ward, and we arranged the beds and furniture in a Pagoda scene with the usual Christmas decorations blending in with it. I had reflective scenes with mirrors, and swans made from pipe cleaners, it was fascinating to see it all taking shape. Elsie in the meantime, had dyed my pyjamas blue with a long fitting blouse and loose sleeves where I was able to fold my hands up my sleeves. I looked like a mandarin with hat accordingly, I used Acriflavine solution on my face to bring me out in a yellow tan, and looked very effective. The Lady Mayoress of Chelmsford came round to see the ward together with Council Officials. I approached her from the ward entrance and in my appropriate short steps went forward to greet her lowering most graciously, and in my best Chinese-English phrases took her round to meet the patients. She seemed very impressed and congratulated all the nursing staff, who had helped me and of course the matron, doctors and nurses were delighted. I was not recognised as male nurse Corkery and were awarded second prize for the best theme. We were all delighted, I remained in my Chinese gear all day, had lunch with patients on the ward. In the afternoon we were allowed to visit the other wards in the hospital, and with glasses of sherry presented to me on each ward, I succeeded in carrying mistletoe with me and greeted all the nurses in the usual festive way by kissing them under the mistletoe. I went on to one female ward, where there was a tall young sister rather prim and proper and somebody dared me to kiss her under the mistletoe. This challenge I accepted, and I could not reach her height, but succeeded in tipping on toes and we both fell onto the empty bed, her hat flying off her head, and there was a great laugh in the ward, patients and staff alike. I took a discreet departure bowing graciously to her, and she kept saying "Who is that Chinese man that kissed me", she was really off her guard, but relaxed into the atmosphere of the Christmas Spirit. I don't know if she ever found out who it was, but it was the talk of the hospital that day, and I had succeeded apparently where young doctors had failed, all nursing staff gave up Christmas day to be there, to be with patients on Christmas. I had been to midnight Mass, so I was able to be free, it was customary for all nurses to be there to give the patients a feeling of home, and particularly the long stay patients. We usually got time off in lieu of being on duty at Christmas. So it was my treat to be with Elsie and the children on this day. Elsie and the children had been to Mass and then her Dad used to take them up to her Mum's place for Christmas dinner, I spent some six happy years at St. John's Hospital.

As I am relating these stories from memory, another time I was on night duty for three months and after settling down the patients, we had a young Irish Sister who came to do her rounds, and one night we put sugar on the corridor so that we would hear her coming, and all of a sudden we heard a heavy creaking step coming and the sugar was being crushed, I looked out and it was Canon Wilson coming round the wards to tell us he would be bringing Holy Communion round in the morning. "Simon" he says "Has somebody spilled the sugar", poor man, he was trying to pick his steps. I told him that we were expecting Dolly as the night sister's nick name was not known to him. He had a good laugh. I told him what we had done, he says "I have just come out of a hot place and trying to pick my steps here made it worse. He looked very warm and I made him a cup of tea and sat him down in a comfortable chair. "What hot place have you been to Father". He says "I have been visiting prisoners in Chelmsford", this was his sense of humour shining through, this was his devotion to duty that even at 10 p.m. he was still carrying out his priestly duties.

Another episode in my memories was the Deputy Night Sister — a male nurse or charge nurse would be a better term, — was on duty on the eve of April fools day, so he dressed up in a female nightie, and got himself pushed on a trolley to the Gynae. Ward with some female haemorrhage,. (he) or she was supposed to have, and got somebody to phone the duty doctor to tell him he had an admission in the ward, it was something like "Carry on Nurse" on the B.B.C. This was about 2 a.m. a trolley was all set up for a drip to put up blood. The doctor started asking the usual embarrassing questions, and having taken the blood pressure, he noticed how hairy the arms were. He suddenly realised, but kept quiet and asked the staff nurse to bring him a 20cc syringe of paraldehyde and prepare him or her for operation. The doctor realised he did not have to go any further, for your man jumped from the bed, through the swing door and could be seen running across the lawn in the transparent nightie.

We all enjoyed working with Ron as he was known and he was very popular on night duty especially the nights he was in charge. In the female ward opposite us they had a heavy ward, so the nurses used to get the trolleys ready with incontinence sheets and draw sheets, and the "Billy" as it was referred to was for the soiled linen, so the nurses started in the far end of the ward and they filled the "Billy" with bedpans and put a sheet across the top of the bag or "Billy" which was on wheels and dragged after the trolley. At about 4 a.m. Ron slipped in where the "Billy" was all filled up with bedpans and removed each one and put them back on the rack and then got into the "Billy" himself and put the sheet over himself. At about 4.30 a.m. this big Irish nurse and her friend started the back round, with just the side light on beside each bed, pressure areas treated, washing and preparing them for a cup of tea at 5 a.m., temperature taken etc. etc. and of course producing a bed pan as well. The Billy was dragged in as well, and when this nurse went to take off the sheet, Ron rose to his full height with the sheet round him and the nurse nearly went mad.

I had an orderly named George with me, who had been a waiter on board ships and had been on several cruises, he was a brilliant orderly, quick, efficient and on the surgical ward where we both worked as a team, he was the best orderly I had the pleasure of working with, we worked especially on the aftercare of patients after operations. It was a thirty bedded ward, and we had all kinds of surgery, Prostatectomies Partial Gastrectomies, you name it, we had it as well as drips, injections, washouts and the usual care of patients as well. I was in charge of the ward and did all the injections, blood pressures, dressings, ward report at 2 a.m. again at 7.45 a.m. These nights I never left the ward except for about twenty minutes when the night sister would relieve me for supper. George would do all the preparations of bread for breakfast, change incontinent patients, urine bags, temperatures if I was in a hurry, he would do the teas in the morning, he used to line them up his arm and put them on the patients lockers, and never spill a drop, he was so used to being a waiter. He was very hygiene conscious, which was a great asset to me on the surgical ward. With his high intelligence, he should have done his training as a male nurse, he was so efficient he used to work part time in one of the hotels in Chelmsford as well, because wages were so poor at that time. One night he came in very worried as it was his wife's birthday next morning and the shops would not be open in time for him to get a nice bunch of flowers. So I mentioned this to a few nurses during my supper break, so they went round the bathrooms where all the flowers were stacked ready for the day staff coming on in the morning, as flowers absorb so much oxygen that they are all removed off the wards, at the visiting time. Anyhow, the nurses got a lovely bouquet of flowers from the mortuary where fresh flowers had been left by the bereaved visitors of patients who had passed away, and even provided a label, with his wife's name on it, so he was a proud man going home that morning on his bicycle.

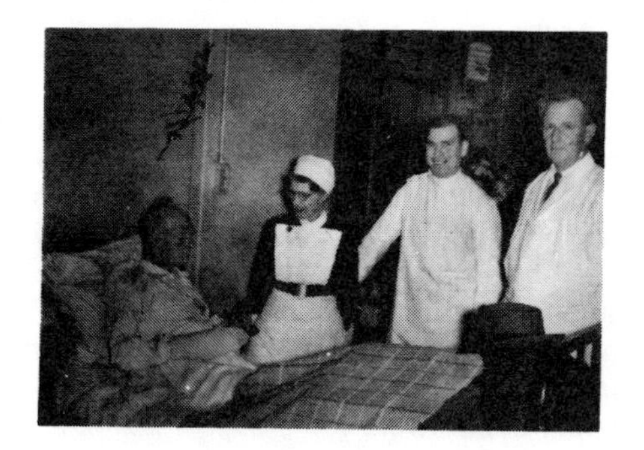

St. John's Hospital
Myself with Sister Hammand
and Jim Sillet

Monsignor Wilson

CHAPTER XII

On April 29th, I had a letter from Fr. Treamer A.A. who was now Provincial of the Order at The Assumption Priory, Victoria Park Square, in Bethnal Green, London E2. I had made contact with him through one of our friends who used to attend our 'Sword of the Spirit' meetings in Jerusalem. He was our R.A.F. Chaplain when I was stationed in Jerusalem before flying to Sicily.

Matron Hynes was now Matron of Broomfield Hospital near Chelmsford where Elsie and myself first met. She was my ward-sister in the Brook General Hospital a few years earlier. She was delighted to meet us again, and together, we arranged for Fr. Treamer to visit us and address the Catholic Nurses Guild. He gave us all a great talk on Jerusalem and the Holy Places, of our former association and of our times together. It was a wonderful reunion for me, and of course we settled down talking with Elsie afterwards and he brought us some Lourdes water for John's rash.

I heard from Fr. Treamer many times after that, but when I moved to the Isle of Wight to live somehow our correspondence ceased and we lost touch. However at the time of writing, I have got the new address of Fr. Treamer from some of his friends in Cork and he is still alive and well in Nottingham Thank God; so I hope that I will be able to meet him again personally one day soon.

The doctor advised Elsie to go out in the fresh air, as she was looking very pale. She went out into the fields pea-picking for a couple of days. This was the annual pursuit in the months of June and July where we lived. We had planned an evening out together on Elsie's birthday, which fell on the 14th of June. However, this was not to be, because she came home from the fields on that day with a very severe throat infection, which of course altered everything, more than we were to realise at that time.

A home help was appointed to help run the house, as Elsie was very sick and had to spend time in bed. John the eldest had picked up impetigo at school, and what with the eczema, the two infections together were driving him crazy, and made a lot of hard work, changing dressings. The doctor sent him into hospital for treatment. Elsie gradually worsened, and her limbs were too sore to stand the pressure of the bedclothes. It was decided she too must go into hospital, but what to do about the children was a real problem. The only answer was to send them into a home, and so the social worker came, and Elsie, tears in her eyes at the thought of the children going away, directed the packing of their clothes, ready for their departure.

When I came home from work, Elsie was sent by ambulance to St. John's Hospital. By the time she arrived there, she had lost the power of her arms and legs, and three different consultants were called to her bedside. After tests and much consultation, her complaint was eventually diagnosed as Polyneuritus.

This was followed by treatment, and much sticking in of pins to see which parts of the body could feel, and which could not, and indelible pencil crosses to show which pricks were felt. She began to look like the tattooed lady at the fair.

It was my unfortunate task to take Angela, Eileen and Elizabeth to the children's home, which was near Colchester, many miles away. It broke my heart to part with the children, and Elizabeth barely a year old, crawled after me, saying "Daddy, Daddy, Daddy," and Elsie's brother who had gone with me, had to help me take her back up the steps and hand her over to a nurse.

John was still in the Isolation Hospital, where he had to have constant treatment for his skin condition. I was in charge of my own ward, while the ward sister was on leave, and I had to arrange off duty for the nurses, and see to everything. My father-in-law was in a different hospital, following a stroke, so between visiting three hospitals, and running a ward, and my children thirty miles away in a home, I was kept rushing around.

I was thrown off my moped, and next day, I was feverish, running a temperature, and had a pain in my chest, so the next door neighbour called an ambulance, and I was admitted to a private ward, across the corridor from where Elsie was in hospital. I shall always remember June 1959 as the darkest time in my married life.

I was diagnosed as having pneumonia and I remember having a huge dose of penicillin, I think seventy-five injections in all. Elsie started to recover, and as she could not walk at this stage, the nurse used to push her over to visit me in the wheelchair, and with a large "Do Not Disturb" notice pinned on the door, they would leave us together. This caused a great laugh. The ward sister was Sister Logan, who I had worked with before and who had looked after me so well, when I was admitted for treatment for an ulcer.

Canon Wilson, "Lord have mercy on him" used to come and see me. He said "Simon, you will have to pray harder!" Not realising what I was going to say, I said "Father, how much more do you think I can take?" I was sorry afterwards for speaking like this to such a lovely man, and such a saintly Priest. I cannot remember whether I apologised or not, but I took his advice and continued my prayers. "Simon" he said "Always remember that God never sends troubles to people, except he knows that they have His grace to overcome it, and accept His will.

The Knights of St. Columba visited Elsie and myself, and they arranged for some of the Knights in Colchester to visit the children in the home. We were several weeks apart and then we were sent to another hospital to recuperate and John was with us. The hospital had lovely grounds, and as it was beautiful weather, we were able to all be together for a lot of the day playing with John outside. Elsie was now able to walk again, I was better and at last the great day came and we were allowed to go home, to try and pick up the threads of family life again.

To be at home felt very strange after being several weeks away. We had a couple of days alone, to prepare us for the great day when we could go to the children's home to be reunited with Angela, Eileen and Elizabeth, who by now had gone past her first birthday, and was taking her first steps.

It was now, well into August, and the first sight of the children was very strange, they seemed to have grown so much, they looked so different, we were nervous that they might have grown away from us, but they were delighted to see us, and ran to greet us. They had been very well cared for, and enjoyed the visits from the Knights, and had been taken to Clacton to the beach. They had learned to mix with the other children, and Eileen cried, because she wanted to bring her special friend — a little coloured boy by the name of Ino — home with her. It took a while to convince her, that he had to stay there. Angela still recalls her time in the home, she had been like a little mother, protecting the other two if any of the other children disturbed them. She was very concerned about Elizabeth who had been trained away from her bottle and had been allowed to cry herself to sleep. This was an awkward situation the first week at home, but she soon settled down again. I myself found it very difficult to settle down. Although we were all united, I could not settle in again.

We were approached by the Social Services about Elsie going on holiday to the seaside and about family planning. I felt if the sea air would do Elsie good, it would benefit all of us if I could get a job at the seaside. I applied for a job in the "Nursing Mirror" in a hospital near Cromer in Norfolk. Canon Wilson was 100% behind my thinking.

It was at this time the Catholic Women's League organised a pilgrimage to Our Lady's Shrine in Walsingham in Norfolk and Elsie, myself, John and Angela went on the coach. We had a lovely day at Our Lady of Walsingham shrine, which is visited by all denominations. It is visited like the Irish people visit Knock shrine in County Mayo. It was a spiritual uplift to Elsie and myself, after all we had been through during those past months. Elsie was completely carried away, and kept everyone in the coach waiting, while she was still writing petitions to leave at the Shrine. She prayed hard, for work at the seaside for me, a new home and another son.

Shortly after the Pilgrimage to Walsingham, the Knights of St. Columba, Council 302 of Chelmsford, arranged their annual dinner dance. We hadn't thought about going at all, but we were in for a big surprise. The Knights arranged for us to have tickets for the night and provided a baby-sitter for us. I shall always be indebted to the Knights for the hospitality and fraternity they showed to my family. We had a wonderful night out, and one of the young Knights announced his engagement to a lovely Irish girl.

Alas, next morning they set off for a motorcycle ride, and had an accident with a bus. They were for some reason, not wearing their head gear, and the girl died in hospital and the young man was unconscious for weeks. The young man was living in a flat near to us and his parents were staying there to be near the hospital. The father was at this time working in Norfolk, so we called at the flat, to ask him what Cromer would be like if I could get a job there. As it happened, the parents were at the hospital, but we told their friend in the adjoining flat, why we had called. He said "Didn't you know they are trying to sell a house on the Isle of Wight, they want to come to Chelmsford to live."

Elsie had been to the Isle of Wight on holidays, and thought it was a lovely place, and wanted to find out more about the house there. We spoke to the mother about their house, and she told me it was beside St. Mary's Hospital in Newport, and that I should apply there for a position. One discussion led to another, and in my mind there seemed to be a way out at last for my ambition to be realised and the prayers Elsie had offered up to Our Lady at Walsingham were in some mysterious way connected to our future.

I said I would swap houses, and use the one solicitor, so after seeing Elsie's parents, we discussed it. Elsie's mother was naturally not keen, as they were responsible for us having a home of our own. I visited the Isle of Wight and saw the house. It was smaller than the one we had, it was at the end of the terrace, on the main road and about five hundred yards away from the hospital. I saw the stained glass window of Our Lady of Lourdes in the front door, and I was so impressed with that, at first sight, that I knew this was what I wanted, and I was sure Elsie would too, but I did not think Elsie's mother would appreciate it.

I had applied for a job to the Matron there, and when I returned I was overjoyed, but did not give all the details to Elsie's mother as I thought she might stop the exchange going through. I took my chance and we moved to the Isle of Wight on November 28th, 1959. Elsie was full of anticipation and apprehension as we made the long train journey, and the children were very excited, although I suppose they hardly realised what was happening. It was a lovely day and it was a new experience for them to go on the ferry.

The weather changed as we reached the Island, and by the time we reached Newport, it was raining.

Our furniture had gone ahead of us, by road, and when we arrived the removal man, had the door off its hinges, and our furniture was piled up outside the door, while the owner's furniture was being brought out, and piled on to the same removal lorry, to go back to Chelmsford. Every where seemed to be in chaos.

Elsie went quickly round the house and of course she was used to larger rooms and more accommodation space. She burst into tears and said "Is this what you have brought me to?" We were all hungry at this time, so we went to a nearby cafe and as it was Friday, we had a nice meal of fried egg and potatoes. As we ate we thought someone was whistling after the girls, we all looked around, and the children soon discovered the Minah bird in the cage, which was to become a great attraction for them, especially Eileen.

Lunch over, and all feeling better, we returned to the house which by now looked far more organised. The removal men left and we settled ourselves in, one of the neighbours helping us, and making us tea. I was lonely leaving Elsie to cope with the new house and the children on her own, but I had to return to Chelmsford to stay with Elsie's mother, while I worked my notice out, at St. John's Hospital. I travelled back that evening and when I told Elsie's mother of Elsie's reactions to the house on the Island, she stormed at me, and made me feel very guilty about the change-over.

Next morning, I was off to work, wondering what was happening on the Isle of Wight, but I soon received a letter from Elsie telling me that she changed her mind completely and was very happy there. She had written it the night of my return to Essex. She'd had the furniture in place and it seemed like home, a girl from down the road, had brought in a large bouquet of flowers, and welcomed her to the community and the children were fast asleep in bed. Elsie's mother was much more pleased when she heard all of this. I was relieved at this news, and I had also received a letter from the Matron of St. Mary's Hospital, asking me to come and see her when I had settled on the island. This was great news, but of course I still had to be interviewed.

I was working on Ward 6 again, on my return from the Island and the nurses were asking me all about the Isle of Wight, and although they would be sorry to see me go, they were delighted we were making a new life for ourselves.

The time passed quickly, and one morning while Sister Logan was at coffee break, I was giving out the ten o'clock medicines when one of the patients stood up to make a speech to say that I was leaving, and that they would like to present me with a little money towards my journey, as a token of their gratitude to me for services rendered, wishing me every success and happiness in my new venture, from all in Ward 6. All their signatures were given to me with the presentation. Sister Logan had come in at this moment, and when she saw the patient, who was getting over a heart attack, out of bed making a speech, she looked at me very seriously, I believe there was applause as well. I have still got that letter to this day. Nurses are not allowed to accept money gifts, but book tokens or chocolates, and usually if a patient feels grateful to a certain nurse, the money is given to the Sister-in-Charge, and it goes to provide some comfort towards the nurses day room. It is not the value of the contents, but the effect it has on you personally as a nurse — you are aware of the gift God has given you in bringing comfort and healing and dignity to this great profession. I was overjoyed to be leaving for another hospital, but I had been so seriously ill myself as a patient there, as had also my wife and son, that I owe a lot, to the nursing skills of that great hospital. I had six years there as a male nurse, and many happy memories as well as sad, but I hope I was helpful, not only in the recovery of my patients, but helping those who passed on. I was alone with them on many occasions and with them in their last moments, when I would bring my expertise, to making their passage from this life to crossing the great divide, which awaits each and everyone of us. I hope they are receiving their Heavenly reward, and that some where behind that curtain, someone will remember me in their prayers.

One of the last eventful happenings before I left the hospital was a flood. There was a freak thunderstorm, the like of which had not been witnessed before — lightning shot through every part of the sky at the one time, lighting up the countryside. There was a strange feeling in the air, and everyone was outside watching the phenomenon. When the storm broke, the floods rose rapidly, and I had to stay overnight at the hospital, there was no possible way of getting home. Wards had to be dried out, and a lot of havoc was caused. The staff of the hospital were marvellous and worked round the clock to keep everything moving. It was about the only time in the history of the hospital that anything like this had occurred. I would say that even at this moment, a new hospital will be built in the area.

WARD 6. CHELMSFORD. HOSPITAL
NOVEMBER 30TH 1959

AS YOU ARE AWARE, OUR FRIEND MR SIMON CORKERY IS LEAVING US THEREFORE WOULD THOSE PERSONS WILLING TO SUBSCRIBE A LITTLE PRESENT FOR HIM, PLEASE SIGN BELOW.

Ward 6
St Johns Hospital
Chelmsford
30-11-59

Simon
Wishing you all success and happiness in your new venture
From all in Ward 6

Ryde Pier

CHAPTER XIII

I arrived back on the Isle of Wight after my notice had expired, and I still had three weeks annual holiday to come. In the meantime I called to see Miss White the matron, and her first words were "When can you start?" I told her I had three weeks holiday to come. So it was that I had succeeded in getting a position and Matron told me to call to the Linen room, where my uniforms were awaiting me. My references that I had with me were not wanted, Matron had already been in touch with Matron Reynoldson, who must have given me a very strong recommendation. I was overjoyed and I asked her for a position for a ward orderly to make a bit of money during my three weeks holiday. "No, certainly not" was the reply. This is your opportunity to have a good rest, so that you will be able to give good service in my hospital.

Matron was kind, homely and indeed a good administrator, as I was to learn in the years that followed. My wife could not believe it, as I walked through the door. "That was a short interview" she said. She just could not believe it at first. We were both happy Thank God, because it was the first time in my nursing career, that I had taken a chance to apply for a job and moved my family, before acceptance. I thought of the advice Canon Wilson had given me about accepting The Will of God and praying harder. We owe a great deal of gratitude to Our Lady for guiding me through stormy waters over a sad period of our lives together. From then on, I was determined to remain closer to the practice of my religion, than I had done previously, although I never went far away, and I thank God for the graces he provided me with.

Our funds were getting low because of the cost of removal etc. We were approaching Christmas and I struck up a plan in my mind to get a job for a couple of weeks. When I had it all thought out I told Elsie about it. I was to change my name to James O'Brien which really was part of my name, and I was to be a medical student who wanted a temporary job to help cover fees. I took the bus to Ryde and went by boat to Portsmouth. I had the address of two hospitals in Portsmouth, and I walked into the first. I asked if I could see the matron, I rehearsed it all in my mind, and I knocked gently on the door, and when I was told to come in, I was so nervous, that I must have suffered some sort of shock instantly, for a voice shouted out "Corkery, what are you doing here?" I was shattered, I forgot my O'Brien, my story about the medical student on hard times, and everything else. It took me a few seconds to compose myself, and tell the owner of this voice that I had left St. John's Hospital and that I was starting nursing in St. Mary's Hospital on the Isle of Wight. I was talking to the assistant matron of the hospital, and she was none other than the Home Sister who had been at St. John's Hospital with me, she had left about a month before I had. Anyhow, I told her truthfully that I was looking for a temporary positicn to get a bit of money to put us through Christmas. She was lovely to me and said she would ask the matron, when she saw her, and let me know. I know that most matrons are committed to stick to the rules, but I did get a letter from her and it was as I had expected, in the negative, but she wished me every success.

Elsie had an uncle staying in Portsmouth, he was working on an extension at "Sainsbury's" and on the day of the interview, I located him, and he was delighted to see me. I gave him our address, and he came on the boat, and arrived on the bus, which stopped across the road from our house. We were very lucky, as well as the buses, we had a train service at the bottom of the hill, and the children were crazy to go on it. The farmer's field and our garden at the back of the house overlooked the railway line, where a steam engine and three carriages used to chug along backwards and forwards to West Cowes. The railway line ran along by the riverside where you could watch the boats laden with timber and grain come up the river to unload at the Quay of Newport. Small sailing boats were often on the river as there was a sailing school nearby and altogether this made a very pleasant view.

I was not able to find employment, but Elsie succeeded in getting a temporary job for a few weeks before Christmas, in Woolworths in Newport, and I looked after the children. She worked on the handkerchief counter and earned £5 per week, so you can tell from that, what wages were in 1959.

Around this time, just before Christmas, the Church had its annual Christmas bazaar. We all went along, and everyone greeted us as newcomers, and made us feel extremely welcome and as though we belonged. This helped us to quickly adjust and settle in to our new surroundings and make new friends, as we virtually knew no one, when we arrived on the shores of the Isle of Wight.

I started nursing on St. Catherine's ward, a geriatric unit, we had a very nice ward sister and some very good orderlies, who were very kind to the patients, and had a great routine worked out. I had to tread my way gently at first, and produced my own nursing skills, that no short cuts were taken. It was heavy going at times, and I was next in charge of the sister downstairs and another male nurse, had his own staff upstairs. Upstairs was known as Totland Ward, the wards in the hospital were all named after places on the Isle of Wight. Matron White took a great interest in all her staff and patients and as she did the ward round with us, she gave the same interest to her elderly patients as she did to those on the acute wards in the "Top Hospital". The hospital consisted of two main blocks, one near the main entrance — the "Bottom Hospital" and the other block, up a slight hill in the grounds, was referred to as the "Top Hospital". The assistant matron was very nice also, a very refined sort of person, and they made a good team, and the staff were very happy.

I was not long at the hospital, when I was asked to take charge of the Catheter Clinic in the Outpatients department. Elderly patients who were not medically fit enough to have surgery for enlarged prostrate glands, had to have their catheter changed every three weeks. Bernie Bloomfield had his patients, and I had mine, so that made a nice change from the ward routine. With the team of orderlies that we had, work went very smoothly. I used to go to the "Top Hospital" for my meals, so I got to know most of the staff during my meal breaks. We had lovely gardens with a boating lake with ducks on it between the "Top Hospital" and "The Bottom Hospital" Matron White was very interested in the lay-out of the grounds, and her knowledge of gardening was her chief hobby. In her off duty periods, she would be seen, talking to the gardeners, and discussing every detail with them. Matron was also, someone like myself who had gone through the medical corps, during the war, and one of the orderlies, who worked with me, was a sergeant with her, in those days, and they were very close. I think she respected me for my part in World War II, and the experience I had gained.

The Isle of Wight is a beautiful island. It is a great holiday resort, and people begin coming to the Island in April. The school children, from London and elsewhere come and do their history, geography and nature study, and it all comes in, as a holiday, educationally orientated. They have the open air and the lovely beaches, and you will see the children clutching their books, returning to the hotels with their teachers about six o'clock, starving hungry. They vacate the hotels on Saturday morning, ready for another school to move in later during the day.

In May, you then have the Senior Citizens, arriving for holidays at cut prices, and from then on, the season continues, full steam ahead, till mid-September. We used to meet a lot of Irish staff in the hotels, especially from Waterford.

I succeeded in getting a job, doing washing up, in the Lincoln Hotel in Shanklin from 6 p.m. till 12 p.m. With the permission of Matron, I got my duties arranged, so that I started at 7.30 a.m. and worked until 5 p.m. I bought a new moped, a N.S.U. Quickly, on the hire purchase, so that I would have good transport. As I reached our house, I would have a few sandwiches and a cup of tea in my hand, often outside the door and then dash off to Shanklin, getting there about six o'clock. Work was non stop from then until nine o'clock. As I went in, all racks were full of trays of ware, that had come from the cafe, and even more, which had come from the beach, as beach trays were provided for people to take away their tea to the deckchairs across the road. These trays were very sandy and often teapots and jugs would be full of sand, left by children who had been allowed to play with them. There was no machine washing, they all had to be rinsed out, washed up properly and then plunged into a sink of boiling water to sterilize. At nine o'clock I would have a meal and the rest of the time was usually not so hectic, as I prepared the potatoes for the following day, ready for the chips, and this was done by machine, just picking the eyes out by hand. This finished by midnight.

If the weather was nice, I would go for a swim, because the water would still be warm, after the heat of the sun during the day. One night, I went for a swim, leaving my clothes in a pile on the beach. I was in the water when all the street lights went out and there was no moon that night. I came out of the water and strolled over to where I knew my clothes were. Standing over the clothes with a torch was a policeman. I got a fright and I expect he did too, no doubt he thought someone had drowned, and was relieved to find me fit and well.

Mr. Murray was my boss and I was paid every Friday night, half a crown an hour. Mrs Marshall owned the hotel, she was a nice person who worked hard all her life to get to the top. Whenever things were busy she would come and give a hand, she was very organised and really kept things moving. When the end of September came and the season finished. I would go to the Hotel on my day off from the hospital to help clean up and put everything away for the following year.

I worked there for several seasons and later on Elsie and the older children took their turn as well, Elsie working in the kitchen, and the children collecting trays, cleaning down tables and generally helping where needed. It was all great fun, as well as hard work, one met so many different people and made many friends, both among the staff and the visitors. There were many different types, who came to work at the Lincoln, they came from all parts, Liverpool, Birmingham, Dungarven and of course the local islanders, some would return regularly every season. One old soul we had, we knew used to take home bits and pieces of food, so one night we took her bag and put two bricks inside of it, and she carried it the whole twelve miles home on the bus, before discovering why it was so heavy.

One lad fancied himself as a Country singer and on his off duty would come and try out his songs on us, much to our dismay, and he was inevitably run out, only to come back again at the next opportunity. One elderly man who was a perfectionist in the still room used to be easily offended, and if someone annoyed him, he would be off home, declaring he would never set foot inside the place again, about an hour later being comforted and cajoled he would be back again, picking away at his lobsters and dressing his crabs as happy as ever, I think he had been there about as long as the hotel had. Really they were a great team, and everyone enjoyed the season even if at times like August Bank Holiday when everyone got very tired tempers became a bit frayed with the heat and the extra work. A Guinness all round from the management soon counteracted this, but the work was hectic at times.

One day during the end of August in 1961, when I was working at the hotel, I had a phone call from Elsie's brother asking for her to go Essex, where her father was dying. I dashed home on the moped, only to find an empty house. Luckily there was a note on the table, saying that as it was such a hot day, Elsie had taken the children to the beach at West Cowes, and would be catching the train back in time for tea. Off I went to West Cowes, calling in at the railway station and was very relieved to find the family there awaiting the train. Back home again Elsie quickly threw a few things into a bag and rushed off to Essex taking Simon the baby with her. Unfortunately, she was just a few minutes too late, but things do not always work out the way we would like them to.

However, there was to be a happier time in October that year when Elsie's sister Audrey got married. We did not get to the wedding, but they came to the Isle of Wight for their honeymoon, and later came to live near us for a while, where they had their first baby daughter.

The winters of 1961-62 went by very quickly, but I did suffer from Bronchitis from time to time, and I still had the occasional bleed and vomiting. One night I was taken really bad, and the pain was so severe and I was vomiting coffee grounds. I put up with the pain for a while, and Elsie was shy about calling the doctor but eventually I felt so bad I wanted to fetch the doctor myself. Elsie eventually phoned the doctor as it was getting daylight and when he arrived and found me in so much pain, he was cross for not calling him sooner. He gave me a shot of morphine which sent me off to sleep, but my head was spinning, and thr room was moving I thought. The doctor put me on medicine for my stomach and made an appointment for me to see Dr. Harland, the medical consultant, who had me x-rayed. They found I had a gall stone, which had travelled down into the bile duct. I then had to see Mr. Gordon Walker, the surgeon. This man I knew, because I had now been working on the surgical ward at the "Top Hospital" where I was under Sister Shergold from West Cowes. She too had been in World War II, so again I was with people, with whom I had something in common.

Easter 1962 and Easter week, I will remember it always! Mr. Gordon Walker said he would not be able to operate, until he came back off leave, but there was an Egyptian Surgeon standing in for him, and he recommended him to me, and told me that I would be in good hands. I was put in a side ward, off the main ward, and all the patients were very concerned about me — patients I had seen through their own operations. I had built up a great rapport with Sister Shergold and the Irish sister who was her partner, who was also very efficient. Some of the patients whom I had given preparational treatments before their operations, would have liked the task of returning the compliment by being able to give me a shave, enema etc. Such was the atmosphere of good will and happiness between patients and staff and was in keeping with the efficiency with which this ward was run.

Poor Elsie was so worked up and worried, that Sister Shergold said that after the operation was over, she rang up to see how I was and her voice was trembling. There was nothing malignant Thank God, but they found the stone, a spiky, awkward looking one, but small in comparison to some of the other patients, who were proud possessors of little tins of gall stones beside their beds. I still have got mine somewhere around. When my stomach had been examined, there was evidence of ulcers which had healed, and they told my wife, she had cured me of them, but had upset the gall bladder instead, with all the egg custards and things. I could continue further and say that the prayers Elsie had offered at Walsingham Shrine and the requests that she had written down were responsible for getting me better. I was full of bronchitis after the operation and had to have a lot of antibiotics. I soon recovered and was allowed home, only to have Elizabeth, the three year old sit herself straight on top of the wound which made me see stars. The Knights were very good and arranged convalesence for me in Bournemouth. After a short while when the weather got warm, I did lots of swimming and soon became fit again.

Simon my second son had already been born on October 18th 1960 and on the evening he was born, Elsie said to Fr. Murphy O'Connour our C.C. that Simon was the answer to her request at Walsingham. When she was told about the results of the operation and the ulcers healing she remembered that was another request. It certainly seemed as if Our Lady was guiding us all through the events of our life — we always said the Rosary faithfully during these days, we were not well off, but we always managed to get by.

I suffered badly from Sinusitis and Bronchitis in 1963 and was sent to see Dr Laidlow, the chest specialist who put me on an inhaler and antibiotics. I was sent away from work for about two months. I spent part of the time in St. Joseph's convalescent home in Bournemouth, which was run by the nuns. I had been there after my gall bladder operation for about two weeks, and the sisters were marvellous, especially the sister in charge of the patients, and we were able to attend daily Mass in the chapel. The doctor came in twice a week and we were allowed along the pier for a walk, and the gardens leading to the pier are beautiful. The weather is warmer there as well and a lot of people retire there because the air is suitable for bronchitis and chest complaints. It was like home from home there, and the meals they served were beautiful. We had concerts on Sunday evenings and the local Knights of St. Columba came to visit me, Eileen Hemus, who was with me during the war years in Jerusalem, lived there and worked in the bank so I was taken out to tea and shown the high spots of Bournemouth. Thank God for the nuns who do so much good work, not only in the teaching profession, but also in the nursing profession. In the convalescent home as well as the medical attention, you also had the spiritual side as well, with the recitation of the Rosary at night.

Some time later, Elsie had to have her tonsils out, and I had to take a week of my holiday to look after the family. The children were all sick at the same time, so I did not visit Elsie, but some kind neighbour told her the children were sick, she was really worried and wanted to come home. I remember Fr. Murphy O'Connor called and I had two days growth of beard, and I was rushing around trying to get something light for them to eat, because they had sore throats. Fr. Murphy O'Connor took a £1 out of his pocket and he said "go over to the shop and get some ice cream for those children". I showed him a letter I had from the Presentation Brothers in Douglas Road, Cork, which my father had forwarded to me from Longford. Fr. Murphy O'Connor read the letter — they were looking for donations towards their Chapel fund, and they were appealing to all past pupils — he was himself a past pupil of the college, and his remark was "They should be sending you a donation, not you sending them one. We had a good laugh over it, but actually it was a very nice letter, and brought back memories of the days I spent in West Cork.

The Isle of Wight is almost as green as Ireland and the people have a lovely friendly nature, always willing to help and have a great sense of humour. I was to realise this, particularly during the next few weeks.

Elsie came home after her operation, and just as the children were getting better, Elsie started shivering and running a high temperature. I rang the doctor who told me the best thing I could do was to throw the thermometer away. I stayed beside her all night, keeping a good fire going, pushing fluids into her and tepid sponging her. I was really annoyed with the doctor and I think I reported him to the senior partner. Anyhow he called next morning and having examined her chest, he became very serious and put her on a strong dosage of penicillin as she was still very feverish. He thought she was suffering from Post Anaesthetic Collapse. This doctor was very apologetic when he realised this, and came several days to see her as she was really sick for about a week. The neighbours all rallied round, one to cook, one to wash, one to iron and so on, they were all fantastic, I was able to go back to work, after my so called "Holiday" and another episode in our daily lives was over.

THE LINCOLN

ESPLANADE
SHANKLIN
I.O.W.

Telephone:
Shanklin 2641
Residents 3060

Directors:
Mrs. F.G. Marshall
(Managing)
C. Marshall
J.C. Marshall
J.I.C. Murray

The Beach outside Lincoln Hotel Shanklin

CHAPTER XIV

The children were growing up fast. The Knights had raised enough money through football pools and other events to build a school for the primary Catholic school children in Newport, to save them having to travel to East Cowes. There was already a Private Convent School in Carisbrooke, and that was to close and a new non fee paying school built in the grounds. East Cowes school was not able to accept Elizabeth, who was now old enough for school so we decided to start her off at the Carisbrooke school together with Angela for company, ready to transfer to the new school when it would open. John and Eileen stayed at East Cowes until the school would be finished. The school at East Cowes was in a marvellous situation. Standing on top of a hill, the children could see the sea clearly from the classrooms, and see all the big liners coming and going from the great port of Southampton.

John and Angela had received their First Holy Communion in St. Thomas of Canterbury Church in Newport in 1961 and 1962 respectively. John was very good at Catechism, but was rather small for his age because he still got attacks of asthma at times. Mrs Hogan our very good friend took him under her wing, and showed him how to serve Mass. She used to come to the house and train him and teach him the Latin responses. She was fantastic with the children and took them to Mass in her car on many a Sunday. There was not so much money spent on the children to prepare them for their First Holy Communions or Confirmations, as there was in Ireland. The girls dress and veil outfits would be more costly than the boys clothes, they wore white shirts and shorts, white socks and plimsoles and their school neck tie and a rosette, all of which would do for general use afterwards. The same set did for John's confirmation the same year. The Bishop only came about every five years, so some children were very young indeed. John started serving Mass on Saturday mornings for the Priest. One Saturday morning, I will not forget! John went to change the book from the Epistle side of the Altar to the Gospel side, and he struggled with it, nearly dropped it and put it back on its original position, and then went back to his kneeling position. Fr. O'Mahony glared at him, and moved it himself. The book on the stand was too heavy for John, as he was small and underweight at that time. Fr. Murphy O'Connor was up in the choir loft, and saw it all, he was laughing about it, it probably brought back some happy memories of his own. He saw John after Mass and told him to tell his mother to give him more porridge in the morning.

Angela looked beautiful on the morning of her First Communion and I felt so proud of her. Everyone was admiring her along the street coming from Mass. There were not many Catholics and it was not very often the people would see Catholic children in their First Holy Communion clothes. Her lovely red hair, glistened in the sunlight and I can remember as well as yesterday, that morning. Angela went in to see the old men in the Church Army nursing home at the bottom of Hunny Hill, and they were thrilled to see her, she was radiantly

Elsie and myself after John's First Holy Communion together with Angela, Eileen and Elizabeth.

Angela on her First Holy Communion Day

happy. Her mother had gone on before us with the younger children. Eileen received her First Holy Communion the year after, and I had to get my duty changed at the hospital, so that I could be with her, Angela was missing on this day, as she had gone to Essex to stay with her grandmother, so that she could be bridesmaid at her Uncle Norman's wedding on the day before.

Eileen also looked beautiful and radiantly happy and looked a real Corkery. I did the same for her as for Angela, and walked home with her. Eileen has a charm all of her own, she expresses with her wistful smile, and long haunting eyelashes, she almost reads your very thoughts.

Elsie and all the mothers were tidying up the hall after the First Holy Communion party which was laid on in Holyrood hall on these occasions. The nuns were marvellous and the children really enjoyed themselves. They had jelly and ice cream and sweet cake for breakfast, but what did they care, it was a great novelty, especially as they were fasting from midnight in those days. I remember on one occasion that Elsie, who at this time had been appointed Cook-in-charge at the new school, had made a cake for the First Holy Communion children decorated with a picture of a host and chalice. We have a photograph in our album of the cake being cut by Sister Perpetua. Sister Paul was headmistress of the school. These nuns belong to the Daughters of Our Lady of the Sacred Heart. The novitiate is in Glandore in West Cork, and some of the nuns are now back in Glandore, who taught our children in Carisbrooke.

I shall be making references to these nuns at the end of my autobiography, but it is fitting that I should pay tribute to them on this occasion, as five of my children were taught by them at this school, and my wife spent three happy years in charge of school meals in that same school. It has untold memories for me and I must say as a Knight of the Order of St. Columba and as a parent, that Irish nuns, wherever they go, or are represented in all the Orders throughout England, and where ever I travelled across the world, be it Jerusalem, Rome, Greece, Sicily or Egypt — they are great ambassadors of Irish culture, of happiness and community spirit in the surroundings in which they find themselves. Many a poor family like ours was, will be eternally grateful for their generosity, and it grieves me when I hear remarks in our country that would belittle them in any way.

John, our eldest boy passed his eleven plus examination at this school, and was accepted to attend St. John's College in Southsea as a dayboy. The school was run by the De La Salle Order. Angela passed her examination the next year, and was accepted for the Presentation Convent in Ryde. I decided I would give them a treat and take them on a visit to Ireland, one day soon. The nuns ran a nursery school as well as the primary school. Simon was able to start here when he was three and a half which was not long after Elsie had started working there. For the intervening time Elsie's mother stayed with us and looked after him.

I was doing permanent night duty, at this time, so that if any of the children were sick, I was there in the house, so that Elsie's work did not interfere with their home life, and the happiness of the home in general, the only trouble was that it was not always convenient as I could not get back to sleep if I was awakened too early. The children actually saw more of their mother than most, as they were all together in the one school.

My father died on September 9th, 1964, and I remember well Simon was home that day, and I was resting on a bed in the living room to be beside him. There was knock on the door, and the lad from the Post Office announced that it was a telegram, I was shattered because I had a heavy night on the ward. He read it out to me, it was from Fr. John, saying Daddy had passed away and that the funeral was the next day. I was really shaken, because he was always such a healthy man, and never complained even when he had pain. I went to the pub across the road and the owner gave me a brandy and rang Elsie at the school. She rushed home and set about trying to book me a flight. She went to the travel agents and was told that she would have to book by lunch time, as it was early closing day. Elsie then went to the bank to try to get the money, although she explained what it was for, and although I was paid through the bank every month, they would not give her any advance. She was nearly in tears and they reluctantly agreed, that if she furnished them with our insurance books, they would give her the money for the fare. From there she went to County Hall where the pay office was considerably more helpful and gave her the weeks wages early. When Elsie came home, everything was arranged for my journey and she had the plane tickets. I was numb with tiredness, both mentally and physically. I went and laid down for a while to see if I could get some sleep before catching the boat and train to London. Although I felt shattered, I managed to get to the airport safely Thank God.

There was a phone call for me from Elsie to see if I had arrived as she was so worried about me after watching me go off on my journey in a complete daze. My name came over the loud speaker and my Aunt Maud was in the airport lounge and heard it as well. She had travelled from Chatham, and we were both booked on the same flight, so Elsie's prayers were following me or else my father R.I.P. was guiding me. It was great seeing Aunt Maud again and we were met in Dublin as my sister Kathleen — Sister Mary Annette — had flown in from America, so we all travelled down to Longford by car from Dublin. I was too late to see my father before they put the lid on the coffin, but it was best that I should have remembered him as he was.

A solemn Requiem Mass was offered by Fr. John. He was given that privilege by the Bishop of Ardagh and Clonmacnoise, Bishop McNamee. He was assisted by several Priests from the diocese. I believe Fr. John said there were ninety four Priests present. My father was held in great esteem by the people of Longford, and the length of the funeral must have been two or three miles long. I heard it said afterwards that they were entering the grave yard, while people were still coming away from the Cathedral car park. The funeral passed Stonepark National School where he had taught, and there was a guard of honour, all the way from the school to the graveside. The girls were on one side and the boys the other side, dropping rose petals as the funeral passed and then they followed on behind the hearse.

Although it was a sad occasion for me, the vision of those children following their former teacher will live on as long as my memory lasts, and the offerings that poured on to his coffin from people of all walks of life, which is a custom that was carried through the years. That custom no longer exists and even at that time I found it very strange, as it is a custom not followed at funerals in other parts of Ireland. It seems that it is only at funerals and weddings that we all get together as a family, but Thank God with air fares coming down, and especially now that our young folk are once more leaving our shores in great numbers due to unemployment, there may be more opportunity for them to come home more often so that they can meet their loved ones more frequently in their young lives.

The scourge of cancer had taken four of my nearest and dearest in five years, so I will not dwell on that phase of my life which is now past tense, but remember them all in my Rosary every night as I hope others will do for me, when my turn comes. There is one thing I must mention before I go on with my story is that Fr. John forgot to say the "Dominus Vobiscum" on one occasion during the Requiem, and he was very worried about it. One of the old Canons said to him "I am sure that one Dominius Vobiscum will not keep your father out of heaven and if it does, God help the rest of us!"

Coming back to reality, life carried on, the children progressing in all kinds of activity. They entered carnivals and one year in Newport, the whole family entered and their photograph was taken and it appeared in the local paper and I got a surprise when I went on duty that night, and one of the patients showed it to me. Angela, Eileen and Elizabeth took up stage dancing, and they got on very well at it, especially Angela, who got bronze, silver and gold medals. They all learnt to play the piano as well and did well at the music festival which was held in Ryde each year, and also in their certificate examinations. The girls were in Brownies and when the Queen visited the Isle of Wight on 26th July 1965 they were in a guard of honour by Newport quay where the Queen landed to walk through the town. I donned my war medals and stood with Elsie and a French Priest, Fr. Prudhomme by the Church to see the Queen as she went by on her way to Carisbrooke Castle where she installed Earl Mountbatten of Burma as Governor of the Isle of Wight. During the winter months the girls were involved in pantomimes in different parts of the Island. The pantomimes were very good and they raised a lot of money for various charities.

We had by this time acquired a three wheeled car with a motor cycle engine in the back. We used to pile the children in and take them to the seaside and other places but it developed a wobble in the one front wheel and eventually it wobbled so much, it just had to be given up for scrap. We replaced it with a Reliant Van which was much better. Elizabeth had her First Holy Communion that summer, and like the other girls she looked beautiful and had a wonderful day.

I decided to take John and Angela to Ireland for the Easter Holidays in 1966 and Elsie used the van to take Eileen, Elizabeth and Simon to Essex for a holiday with her mother. We all set off at the same time, and the weather seemed very good. I flew from Southampton to Dublin with John and Angela. Fr. John met us in Dublin and took us by car to Longford, where we stayed with the Conlons, my first cousins, near Ballymahon. By the time we reached there, everywhere was covered with snow. I was worried about Elsie, because she was driving on her own in a very old van with three small children, and another one soon to be born, but she had managed to reach her destination before the snow got too bad.

John Conlon and his wife Phyl had a young family also, and we were made very welcome, they took us around everywhere and Angela got on very well with their girls, especially Marcella. Father John took us to see his old pal from his years in Maynooth — Mel Lyons. I showed them my mothers grave while we were in Ardagh visiting Mel. We went to see my brothers and sisters in Longford, and my step-mother, who made us very welcome. This holiday was a treat because they passed their eleven plus exam and they also topped the school for Religious Knowledge and were awarded certificates by the Knights of St. Columba, who sponsored the award. I had promised them that I would do this the year before. We had a great fortnights holiday, there was snow on the ground for much of the time, but this did not spoil anything.

President gives Ardagh his seal of approval

Ardagh Village — Winner of Tidy Towns Competition 1989

CHAPTER XV

Back home again after this pleasant break, we settled down again once more. In the early hours of the morning of June 25th, our daughter Sarah Jane was born. Elsie's mother was staying with us to mind the children and I took Elsie to the hospital, the night before when I went on night duty. I was working on Hassall Ward and around 4.30 a.m. the phone rang, and it was the maternity unit to tell me about the birth. As soon as it was convenient I went over to the maternity ward and what did I see, but my friend John Wright, another male nurse, walking around with my daughter in his arms. "How dare you" I said "take up my daughter with all your old germs off the ward". John and I had been great friends over the years and a marvellous nurse he had turned out to be, and really I was delighted to see that he was taking an interest in the baby. When I went back to the ward, to give out the morning medicines the patients said "We don't want any tablets from you this morning, you might give us the wrong ones, in all your excitement". Of course, they were all congratulating me, and it was a wonderful morning. I went back and spent some time with my wife and baby before going home for breakfast and giving the good news to the family. I remember the ducks coming up from the pond, followed by their ducklings, it looked as though they were all coming to greet the new arrival.

This was Saturday and the next day Sunday was the day that my other three daughters, Angela, Eileen and Elizabeth were to be confirmed. They would all get their confirmation at the one time, as I think I mentioned, the Bishop only came over to Confirm the children every fourth or fifth year at that time. Elsie was disappointed that she would not be at the Church, but I saw the Priest and he hoped to arrange with the Bishop to baptise Sarah, when he was to visit the hospital after the Confirmation. This all seemed fairly certain, but then after the Confirmation the Bishop took sick and had to postpone his visit to the hospitals and prisons, so it did not take place.

Elsie had all the confirmation clothes ready at home and Eileen's God-mother had arrived from Essex to be present, so she was able to see after them, and get them ready. Elsie was allowed home from hospital after lunch that day. She was to come home by ambulance, which was the practice, but in all the excitement she forgot the baby wasn't in the ambulance with her, when they closed the ambulance doors, the nurse who carried the baby out, was still holding her in the doorway of the hospital. One shout and all was rectified, and that was fine, except that the next thing was, the ambulance men tried to deliver Elsie and the baby to the house next door instead of our house. They had her in the wheelchair and nearly to the door, before she could make them understand. With a sigh of relief she arrived indoors and was able to see the girls in their confirmation dresses before they went to Church. I was sponsor to two little boys that day, and all the sponsors were seated beside the children, that they were to sponsor. Bishop Worlock examined the children from his seat at the Sanctuary gates, and Eileen was foremost in her answers, she seemed to blossom forth, eyes shining with happiness. All three girls looked lovely in their veils and were radiant. Another friend who worked with Elsie was sponsor for Angela and Elizabeth and she came back to the house where they helped with the tea, as Elsie naturally was feeling rather weak. His Lordship visited the school at Carisbrooke the next day and he went straight over to Eileen in the classroom, and said "This is the clever little girl, who answered all my questions". So our family would have made history had the Baptism and Confirmation all been on the one day. Sarah's baptism took place two Sundays later. Margery Freeland our friend, who had been Elizabeth's sponsor for the confirmation was Sarah's Godmother. By this time Elsie's sister and her family had arrived for a holiday, so we had another great day.

Looking back on these days, when happiness was complete and to see the joy in Elsie's face, such memorable occasions may only happen once in a lifetime, so it is to be recorded in this book so that my children may remember their youth, and it may help them in the troubles of tomorrow, that seem to blot out the innocence and the great joy they experienced at the coming of the Holy Spirit into their lives.

Confirmation Day Newport June 26th 1966

CHAPTER XVI

By this time the older children were progressing well. Eileen went with Angela to Ryde Convent and Simon had been in the Primary School for a year, they were growing up fast. The money on permanent nights was easing my financial burdens, thanks to the Matron who arranged it for me. I advanced in the nursing field, in the modern advances of medical knowledge, that now loomed on the horizon. Dialysis had come into its own for the people who had infected kidneys and I felt justly proud of having taken the first case in the hospital and specialising in this field. I love specialling patients because it gives you a chance to put forward your nursing skills and bring effective results.

I had occasion to take a little boy to the Odstock Hospital burns unit, who had received severe burns from a boiling kettle. I travelled with him and his mother, by ambulance on the boat, and over to the mainland, and had to keep continuous plasma drips going, stopping on the mainland to change each drip and record on a chart, the pulse, blood pressure and temperature en route. Matron White asked me personally to accompany him, and Thank God, any task she assigned to me, was a success.

Another day, a friend of mine was to be airlifted by helicopter to the Atkinson Morley Hospital in London, for immediate brain surgery. I had been to this hospital before by ambulance, but not by air, so I was delighted when I was asked to accompany him. However I did not get a chance to go after all. I waited all morning for the helicopter to arrive, hoping that it would do so before I went off duty, as it was my half-day for the week. I had to go home without realising my ambition, and another male nurse was chosen to take my place. I was disappointed, and so was the ward sister who knew that I had experience of travelling by air with patients from the Island of Rhodes to Athens and on to Italy during the war years. Later that afternoon, when we were in the park giving swings to the children, I saw the helicopter land and take off from the hospital, and knew that my chance had gone.

I loved my work, and patients would say to me in the morning, when I would start the morning rounds of, temperatures, teas, washes and injections — "How is it, you can keep so cheerful and always smiling, after working hard all night".

I was chosen by Matron White to go on a refresher course to the mainland for Senior Nurses. There were four of us altogether, but I was the only male nurse from our hospital. It was a beautifully run course, and we had a wonderful tutor, concerning procedures in modern thinking in practical and theory. I enjoyed meeting the nurses from the other hospitals and exchanging ideas. The course took place in Winchester, which is a lovely town. In our off duty we used to go out and maybe meet in the local pubs, and have a laugh with the other male nurses. I cannot remember whether the course lasted for seven or ten days, but I know that we had a test on the Friday morning, before returning to the Island. We did not know if this was going to be a hard exam, but as it happened we were all given different things to do. I had to prepare a trolley for a blood transfusion, and explain what each item on the trolley was used for, and in what category. You had to accompany the doctor to the patients bedside, but this was all done in theory as it were, but you had to have the patient's name and notes on the bottom of the trolley. You had to have the Blood Pressure machine etc. You had to mention how many drops per minute and see that the doctor recorded this on your patient's chart, you had to visualise if the patient had to have one pint or two pints of blood. Observance of the drip — whether the arm was swelling near the entrance to the vein, if the blood was going into the tissues, and what you would do if that happened. I had a mental picture framed in my mind of everything that I had to do, and I told the Sister Tutor everything I had put into operation during my years of nursing. When I had finished, she said "I think Mr. Corkery has covered every aspect, and his observance of what he had to do. Nothing was left out". The other nurses were present during all of this and I knew by their smiles, that I had not let the side down. We were taken around a lovely modern hospital in Southampton the following day which we really enjoyed as it relaxed us after our ordeals.

I returned to the Island, and Matron sent for me on Monday morning. As I entered her office, she said "Congratulations Mr. Corkery, you did well on the course, I had a report about you, before you came back to the Island". From then on, I could say I felt over the moon, because it meant promotion to senior work and more money.

The Salmon Report as it was called, came at that time, and was the uplifting and reorganisation of the National Health Service. The ideas of Matrons and Assistant Matrons had gone, and the organisation had altered the whole set up of administration. Uniforms changed, fawn stockings as opposed to black were allowed on duty, even the title of Nurse was almost thrown out the window — staff became Nursing Officers 1-10. Senior Officer No. 9 would be in charge of a group hospital and Senior Officer No. 10 would be in charge of the whole group of hospitals in the area. There was a regular open forum, where nurses could have their ideas listened to, almost like the seminars are run. Nurses over eighteen years, were allowed to live out in flats if they chose, instead of living in the Nurses Home. They were given a whole new status. Believe me, it caused chaos at first. Nurses were encouraged to join a Union, which was alien to my way of thinking. Nurses could get their S.R.N. and put their names down to study for a University degree, and become a tutor. Salaries were improved and shorter working hours adopted. It took a long time for older nurses to adapt to these ideas and people who were near to retiring age, chose to do so early, as they could not accept the new situation. Matron White, herself retired, and we all felt very sad because she had acquired a good nursing staff and ran a very happy hospital. She was up to date in accepting the new ideas, but they came too late for her to be able to get the benefit of them. The female nurses felt they had lost an intimate friend. If you had problems, she was the one to set you straight, and she was strict but very kind. When she left, it seemed like the end of an era.

The new Senior Nursing Officer was Miss Waldron. With all the changes, I had to adapt to new thinking and new ways of approaching people, but I still retained my friendship and loyalty to my patients and I was asked to take over on a Geriatric unit of two wards in the "Bottom Hospital". I told Miss Waldron that I enjoyed working on the acute wards at the "Top Hospital" but she told me that skilled staff were needed for the geriatrics as well, and that as I was a married man with a family on night duty, she would allow me Friday, Saturday and Sunday nights off, if I would take the position. She said "I am in charge now, and I will give you a week to think it over". I decided to take the offer and went to work at the bottom hospital with Sister Groves and another male charge nurse.

Angela and Eileen in the Carnival

CHAPTER XVII

When our baby Sarah was six months old, Elsie once more had to go into hospital for surgery, this time it was for three weeks followed by two weeks convalescence. One of the other nurses and myself shared the responsibility of looking after Sarah. Staff nurse Mew from near Gurnard had her the nights that I was on duty, then I would collect her and have her at the weekend. Another elderly lady came and slept in our house with the other children and prepared them for school in the morning. She was wonderful with them, she was so kind and did a lot of social work for the local prisoners, accommodating visiting wives and minding children for them, while they visited their husbands in prison. Sarah was still bottle fed and a very good baby, so it was easy to change her, wash and do all that was necessary for her. Angela was great with her, and helped a lot with the children as she was nearly twelve years of age.

I was very lucky working with Staff Nurse Mew and finding people as kind as she was to me. This was the loyalty of nurses, to one another who shared the joys and working together, and in times of crisis, helped each other out. I almost forgot to mention that on the day Elsie was to go to Bournemouth for convalescence, I had to pack her case, because she was not allowed home first, as she was to go with a special attendant on the journey straight from hospital.

It was late January, and I told her she had better take her fur coat, such as it was, as people were rather smart in Bournemouth. I packed the coat and took it to the hospital. When Elsie got dressed for the journey, there were suddenly howls of laughter from everyone in the ward. I could not locate the proper pair of shoes, and as next best thing, what had I brought, but a pair of tatty, brightly striped canvas summer beach shoes to wear with a winter fur coat. Elsie remembered where her shoes were, and I made a hasty retreat and returned with the correct ones. Elsie enjoyed her holiday, but missed the family dreadfully. The weather was very kind to her, it was really springlike and she was encouraged to go for long walks every day. I went to Bournemouth to accompany her home, and the crossing on the ferry from Lymington to Yarmouth was as good as any on a summer day. The sun was shining brightly and it was possible to stay on the open deck all the way over.

Elsie's health improved and she went back to working for the school meals service but this time in a school just across the road from our house. A lady nearby, took Sarah while she was working, Elsie collecting her on the way home. This lasted for two years, but then the owner of the cafe where I worked came and begged Elsie to go to work for them from Easter until the end of September. She was rather loathe to do this, because school meal hours were far more suitable. What changed her mind was the fact that my brother Eamonn was to be ordained in June and by working at the hotel, we would be able to accept the invitation, as the pay was much higher. It was agreed that Elsie would get the time off to go to the ordination in June 1968, when the Ceremony would take place in Longford Cathedral.

We took Eileen, Elizabeth and Simon with us, as they had not had the chance of going to Ireland before. We went by boat and train. Elsie's mother came to stay and look after Angela, John and Sarah. We went on the boat that went from Holyhead to Dublin and then by train down to Longford. While I was on this train, I went along to freshen myself up after the long journey. Washing my hands, I slipped off the ring I was wearing and put it on the side of the wash-basin, as soap tended to get caught up on it. Father John had given me the ring as a special gift, which he had brought from Nigeria. I never used it on the wards or in the theatre as we were not allowed to, I only wore it when I was going out. The ring was silver, the shape of a square signet ring, with a gold elephant embossed on it. I went back to the family, and suddenly I realised I had left the ring on the wash basin, I rushed straight back, but when I got there, it had gone. I reported it to the guard on the train and to this day, it has never turned up. I have often thought of getting it mentioned on the Gay Byrne programme to see if anyone is wearing that ring. I don't think my brother believes me, but it took all the joy out of the journey over, because it had been specially designed for me. Maybe if this book is published, perhaps somebody will realise that it is of great sentimental value to me. When Bishop Magee lost that beautiful ring given to him by Pope Paul VI, I can realise and sympathise with him also.

Anyhow, we had a great day at the ordination, and the children really enjoyed it also. I had missed Fr. John's ordination, so this was a wonderful experience to be at Fr. Eamonn's. Father John had baptised him, was present at his Confirmation, and now once again he was able to be there and able to put his hands on his head. It must have been a wonderful experience for both of them, and there has been a great relationship between them ever since. They concelebrated Eamonn's First Mass together as well. It was a great family reunion for Elsie and myself, and of course Baby was delighted and I shall be eternally grateful to her, for her kind invitation.

His Lordship Bishop Cathal Daly ordained Fr. Eamonn, and when we were at the altar rails to meet the Bishop, and when Fr. Eamonn started introducing Elsie and myself, the Bishop said, "I have met Simon and Elsie in London" and turning to us said "How is everything on the Isle of Wight?" That demonstrates what a wonderful memory he has, that in the midst of all this ceremony, he was able to remember so much detail. We had been introduced to him at a Longfordman's Association Dinner in London by Paddy Keegan who worked at the Irish Centre in Camden Town and was Chairman of the Association at that time.

We had a great time meeting the Conlon's on my mother's side and Eileen, Elizabeth, and Simon made great friends with all the other families of Corkerys in Longford. The day we were to go to Dublin for the return journey I called on Theresa Dalton's husband, who kept a double barrell gun, which I had used before on another occasion. Anyhow the cartridges were damp, and jammed a couple of times. His daughter cycled up the road to get another couple, so at the third attempt, there was a jam jar with a lid on it, placed lying down on the gate post. Fr. John was getting agitated at this time, and he said. "Do you know we shall only have an hour to get us to Dublin? I don't believe you could hit a haystack". With that I brought the gun up to my shoulder, and aimed as we were taught to do in the R.A.F. and I blasted the lid completely, and came home triumphant with the lid to prove it.

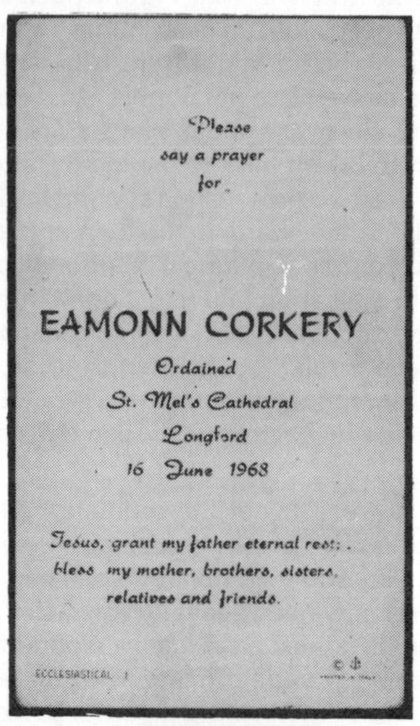

Please
say a prayer
for

EAMONN CORKERY
Ordained
St. Mel's Cathedral
Longford
16 June 1968

Jesus, grant my father eternal rest;
bless my mother, brothers, sisters,
relatives and friends.

Fr. Eamon newly ordained with all his relatives

CHAPTER XVIII

It was a great reunion with Sister Mary Annette, who had been looking forward to Fr. Eamonn's ordination during these hard years of study. We invited them both back to the Isle of Wight for a holiday. They came over and stayed with us for two weeks and the Parish Priest in Newport Fr. Reeves, introduced Fr. Eamonn to the people of the parish, and Fr. Eamonn gave them all his Blessing. Sr. Mary Annette and Fr. Eamonn had a well earned rest, they are great pals, and we were delighted to be able to repay them, in some small way for their courtesy and the honour of having been invited on the auspicious occasion of the Ordination. Fr. Eamonn was Diocesan Examiner to Bishop Cathal Daly for a few years, and has had various parishes since then. At this stage in the family we had two Priests and a Nun, and at a future date you will see that another nephew became a Priest, and I will bring you into that scenario, when this book will be nearing completion, so stay posted.

Elsie and I continued our married life together, bringing up six children. In August 1968 , we sold our house in Hunny Hill and moved to Shanklin. I had seen a house near the Catholic Church in Atherley Road for sale, and I rather liked the look of it, as well as being near the Church, it was convenient to the railway station, the buses and the shops.

One evening I picked up Elsie after her work in the hotel and going up the road, I stopped outside this house. Elsie said "What are we stopping here for?" I replied "I am going to buy that house". She thought I was out of my mind. "How on earth can we buy a big house like that" she asked, but I could see by her face, that she would like to do so. Elsie's mother came to see the house, and she was very impressed, and said it was near to the sea, a clean modern town with a good shopping centre and theatre. There were some lovely walks between Shanklin and Sandown and it was not far from Ventnor which is very beautiful.

Of course I had already met Father O'Riordan, the Parish Priest of Shanklin, as he was chaplain to the Knights. The Church was brand new, and what I call a prayerful Church. It had been bombed during Benediction, one evening, during the war in 1943 and six people were killed and others injured. In 1949 a temporary Church had been built and the present Church was finished in 1957, incorporating a small part of the original Church.

Wheels were set in motion, and we sold our house fairly quickly but this house was more expensive and a lot of negotiation had to be done to raise the difference. The new house cost £4,000, quite a lot of money in those days.

We moved into the house in August, the peak month of the season. The elderly lady we bought it from, told us that she did a lot of bed and breakfast catering, during the season, and that we would be able to do good business. I hadn't thought of using the house for that purpose at this time, I looked on it, as a realy family home at last. It had large rooms, and a nice garden and chalet at the back, and a small garden at the front. One side of the garden was the gable end of the Church Hall and the other side a tall privet hedge, so it was very private. Anyway we had no sooner landed and settled in, than there was a knock at the door, with four people looking for bed and breakfast for the weekend. It was about 10 p.m. and Elsie was very tired after working at the hotel all day and had just settled down in bed. Elsie's mother said "Call her down, there is money waiting for us on the doorstep". We hurried around and brought our guests supper while the beds were quickly made up — and so started our first business venture, for the season at least, and we found that we thoroughly enjoyed it.

Angela and Eileen carried on going to Ryde Convent, as they were able to catch the train, which they enjoyed more than the bus. They both started paper rounds which they did every morning before catching the train, and so were able to pick up some pocket money, which was badly needed and also gave them some independence and a feeling of responsibility.

Elsie's mother loved Shanklin and made it her second home during the years that followed. Elsie invited her school friends on holidays who married around the same time as ourselves and had all been friends of ours in Essex, so we had marvellous summers together and their children were able to play with our children. We gave them an evening meal as well, and then we would go out together in the evening. They usually spent all day, every day, on the beach weather permitting. A great routine had been worked out — they would get up early and make sandwiches and Elsie would fill flasks. The men would then take the food and all the beach gear — sun beds, wind shields, balls, swimming rings — out to the cars and drive the cars down and park them beside the beach about half a mile away, while there was still parking space, and then walk home for breakfast, great exercise for the men, and a great help to the ladies.

Elizabeth and Simon went to school in Ventnor and John was going by boat to the De La Salle School in Southsea, near Portsmouth. The sea crossing was good for John's asthma. He and the others were growing in stature, and the family was alive with activity, homework, swimming, music, youth club and participating in the choir which was started by Sister Mary Mercy, who also taught them to play the guitar, and any other activity that came their way. The house always seemed to be full of their friends, we often used to liken it to a railway station, with all the comings and goings. Sarah by this time was growing up, and had started going to the Nursery School run by Ryde Convent, travelling with the older girls after a while. Elsie used to take her the first few months, fetching her home at lunch time, but she used to cry to stay at school and soon stayed all day, but it was too much for her and she often used to fall asleep in the middle of her tea.

The house was quiet when I used to come home from work in the morning, and Elsie's mother would have a lovely breakfast waiting for me and I could go off to sleep until 4 p.m. when Elsie would come in, and bring me a cup of tea about 4.30 p.m. These years were some of the happiest of our married

LORETTA HOUSE

15 ATHERLEY ROAD, SHANKLIN
ISLE OF WIGHT

The family when we lived in Shanklin

life. The children were going from success to success and very involved in parish life. Elsie was working part time in school meals again, helping at the hotel in the summer holidays. I was kept busy with the Knights of St. Columba work, as I had become very active in the organisation. I became a Minister of the Word, did Church door collections, organised the offertory procession during Mass, and helped see everybody into their seats at the 10.30 a.m. Sunday Mass. This was a hectic job during the summer months, as we had a packed church from May until September. I can remember packing the the congregation in, even up to the altar steps. The Priest had a roof erected between the Church and the hall and then we were able to open the doors at the back of the Church and the congregation was able to overflow into the hall, as the double doors at the back of the Church, and the double doors of the hall were opposite each other, and you could see the altar from inside the hall, so not feeling too cut off. After Mass the hall was used as a place to provide a cup of tea or coffee for those who had to wait for transport home and for visitors, and while it was a great place for making friends and meeting old ones, a small charge was made and the proceeds used to send handicapped children to Lourdes. Elsie used to be playing the organ up in the gallery at the back of the Church, and was able to quietly slip out before the last hymn and switch on the tea urn and then creep back again in time to play for the end of Mass. We had a rota of helpers and we all thoroughly enjoyed it, even in the winter time, the locals used to enjoy going in for a cup of tea and a chat before going home.

Elsie and I had a three wheeler car each, for going to work. I carried on at St. Mary's Hospital on St. Catherine's Ward working Sunday, Monday, Tuesday and Wednesday nights on twelve hour shifts and having Thursday, Friday and Saturday nights off. I hated leaving the family on Sunday evening to go to work, but then, in the morning on my way home, I used to feel great satisfaction in going home, whilst all the other people were tearing off to work in the opposite direction. I used to give one of our ward orderlies a lift home in the morning, and that used to help with the petrol bill. I used to say to her "look at those suckers going to work, and we are going home", especially on the Monday mornings.

The years seemed to go too quickly, I was so busy. I had so much to give in Church Affairs, in Knights activities and I also got involved in politics and joined the Conservative Party, and became a member of the Club in Shanklin, which I still visit today whenever I go to the Island for a few days.

It was during 1970 that my step-mother "Baby" and her daughter Angela, and Angela's husband Tommy and their small daughter Kathleen came to visit us from Longford. It was Baby's first time out of Ireland, and I don't know how they got her on the boat — it was only when they were well out to sea, that she asked Tommy "When are we getting on the boat"? When they told her that she was half way across the Irish Sea she had a great surprise, as she had always had a fear of travel. It was lovely to have had them over for a holiday. Baby, Angela and Tommy were delighted with the scenery, and the facilities at the seaside for the children. Baby was completely taken over by the friendliness of the people, the respect they had when they attended Mass, and she was convinced that there was more sincerity in their prayers, than there was in Ireland. I myself was overjoyed, because she had reared eleven of her own children plus two step-children, in hard times, and one teachers salary was not a lot in those years, especially when they were teenagers. During her visit to the Isle of Wight, there is one occasion I shall always remember and when I think of it now, I cannot help laughing. We all went on the hovercraft that went between Ryde pier and Portsmouth and Southsea. We all settled down on the hovercraft and I was sitting beside her, and as we set off from the shore, I saw her make the Sign of the Cross, and then search for the handbag. In the front seat were a middle-aged couple, and one lady who was wearing a fur coat, and looked as we would say today — in the Yuppie class, sat right in front of Baby. To put you in the picture, the hovercraft moves across the water on an air cushion, and is closed in all round, by perspex or some such compound, like the windows of a bus, which cuts out all draughts. The next thing, Baby took out the Holy Water bottle from the handbag and scattered it all over the people in front as well as behind, and the lady with the fur coat turned to the other couple and in a very cultured Oxford accent said "I have never known the spray from the sea come into the hovercraft before!" Of course by this time all the people on the hovercraft were looking at us. I told the lady in front what had happened, and there was great laughter when they realised it was Baby with her Holy Water who was causing the spray. Even though Baby had survived the boat journey, train journey and hovercraft journey, she was still afraid of the journey home because there was an escalator at Euston Station, which they had used when coming. We travelled to London with them, saw a few of the sights like Buckingham Palace and then went to Euston to protect Baby from the escalator. Elsie walked up the stairs with her on to the station and then she was happy to be safely on her journey home to Ireland.

In October of the same year John flew to Rome with a group to be present at the Canonisation of the Forty Martyrs of England and he told us that Bishop Worlock sat beside him on the plane so he felt highly honoured. The whole trip was a great experience for him. While he was away, there was great excitement in Shanklin for a few days. We were watching television late one night, when a news flash came through that there was an oil tanker in difficulties off the south coast of the Isle of Wight. We got into the car and drove down to the seafront, and in the distance could see the red glow of the tanker on fire. When daylight came we went down to the seafront and the vessel had drifted right in front of Shanklin beach and all the fireboats were out round her trying to quench the flames. It took two or three days and everyone was watching the attempt. Eventually tugs came to tow the tanker away but one capsized on the rocks by Culver Cliff at Sandown where it can still be seen. The burning of the tanker was a great tragedy but slowly life went back to normal and all that was left to remind us was the oil on the beaches and the dead birds covered in oil. The children found a bird one day that was covered with oil, but was still alive.

We took it in to the car and rushed off to the bird sanctuary to try and save it, but it died on Elsie's lap, half way there.

There is a great interest in boating and sailing on the Island and the feat of Alec Rose sailing round the world from Southsea caught everyones imagination. Everyone followed his progress with great interest. He had a great send off from the people of Portsmouth and the Island and when he came home safely, he had a tremendous welcome. Sir Francis Chichester had achieved the same great feat of sailing round the world a few years earlier, but this was nearer home, and so many local people knew Alex Rose personally. A year after his departure, tension was mounting, and everyone was waiting for his boat to reach the Nab Tower. They were all out with binoculars to see who would get the first sighting. It was one of the greatest moments in the history of the Island and Portsmouth and it is an episode in my life that will remain for many years to come.

Elsie was promoted to Cook Supervisor in the new Forelands County Middle School in Bembridge. She had a wonderful staff there and it is with pleasure I now enclose a poem written by Wendy Chick, one of the staff as a tribute to Elsie.

ODE TO THE KITCHEN STAFF
FORELANDS MIDDLE SCHOOL

Worn and weary though we may be
Happiness reigns most certainly,
It wafts across the kitchen floor
And even leaks out of the door,
The whole school can feel the atmosphere
Good job the jokes they cannot hear!
After standing for hours over a red-hot stove
We can always depend on on Mrs. Perrigrove
Her humour may be a little blue
But we thoroughly enjoy it, 'tis true.
Lunchtime passes far too quick
The blame there lies with Mrs. Chick.
She cannot help her laugh I know
But once she starts it seems to grow
First one face spreads and splits with glee
Then another, then two or three
Until we're all quite beyond hope
And all that work with which to cope!
However, we do not shirk our job
Even though it makes us sob,
Greasy tins and burnt-on pans
Plays havoc with our lily-white hands!
But we're not complaining of our lot

Not when there's bubbly Mrs. Scott
Her energy amazes all
And her stamina never seems to fall.
Miss Chick, however, does us no credit
If she talked and ate less, ah! now I've said it!
She can't help her compulsive chatter
Or that she's as mad as a hatter!
Mrs. Corkery has our sympathy
Her patience is plain to see
To control her staff is a difficult task
But she continues to the very last.
One day we'll show our appreciation
Her hard work deserves admiration.
Our part-time ladies suffer too
We leave them all the dishes to do
But do they ever moan or groan
No, not even when they're accident-prone!
Ah! Mrs. Chick and Mrs. Seymore
It hurts us to see your hands so sore
Oh! Mrs Collis and Mrs. Bartrum
What would we do if you didn't come.
Next come the supervisors who have it easy
Though none of us would be so crazy
As to join their daily fight in the dining hall
Oh! Pat and Nicky how do you manage them all?

As you can tell, we're proud of our little firm
But thank goodness for the end of term!!

It was during her stay there that Sir Alec Rose, as he now was, came to officially open the school. Elsie had an official invitation — that was November 5th 1970 at 2.30 p.m. — and she was seen on television later that evening serving tea to Sir Alec Rose and the special guests and teachers.

There was a lot of historic memories connected with the Island. From Egypt Point, between West Cowes and Gurnard, one could get a very close view of the ships leaving Southampton, as they followed the deep water channel that brought them very near to the shore of the Island at that particular spot. I remember being at Egypt Point, when the "Queen Mary" sailed past coming out of Southampton on her last historic voyage to New York, where she had sailed so many times, during the years of peace, years of war, and back again to bring many joys to the many peoples around the world who took part in these voyages. I also witnessed the last voyage of the "Queen Elizabeth" from Egypt Point, and also watched the "Queen Elizabeth and the huge American liner "U.S.A." pass within a few yards of each other. The two great giants of the sea, passing, with darkness falling was a sight to behold as

Sir Alex Rose at the opening of Forelands School Bembridge Isle of Wight

they were reflected in the water with their lights full on and their flags flying, and the huge wash hit the sea wall, as I stood there, realising that these two ships, would never again pass each other so close, with the "Queens" destined to become floating hotels. I have seen many other great liners from that same spot — The "France", the "Canberra" and of course the present giant of the sea — the Q.E. II.

West Cowes in Cowes Week is a wonderful sight. I have seen the yachts at West Cowes during Cowes Week stretched out across the bay in the direction of East Cowes like some huge archway of rainbows stretching its arms in magnificent splendour on the approach of our Autumnal season when the "Ladies of the Sea" and of course the Royal Yacht Britannia passed each other by. At the close of Cowes Week there was always a magnificent firework display to which people from all corners of the Island came by coach, bus car, cycle, any mode of transport just to be there. There was a terrific atmosphere of gaiety, but afterwards a kind of sadness that the main event of the year was over. Of course there was still Ryde Carnival to come, a combination of all the Carnival Queens, and all the best floats, from the carnivals of all the other towns on the Island which had taken place in the previous weeks, followed last of all at the end of the season by the Flood Lit Procession.

Around this time there even greater event took place. Something new at that time — an outdoor pop festival at Totland near Freshwater Bay. Everyone was intrigued with the idea, but not sure whether they favoured it or not, as it was the first time it was to happen. The time of it, coincided with the time we were taking part in student exchange schemes. On two occasions we had Swedish girls for four weeks at a time. They came in pairs and were delightful. Eileen also had her French pen friend Annie to stay, and at the time of the Festival had returned to France with Annie for a months holiday, the actual week of the festival we had another French girl Catherine staying with us. The girls really enjoyed these exchange visits, it was great for them to mix with people from other countries, and I think everyone gained from it.

They all clamoured to go to the Pop Festival, so I took it upon myself to take John, Angela, Catherine the French girl, and another friend of theirs. The site was packed, if you wanted to go anywhere you had to keep together or you would not be able to find your party when you got back. It was a big responsibility taking them, but I felt I had to be there, as there was at that time, the introduction of drugs at different dances, and at gatherings such as these.

I remember well listening to Jimmy Hendrix, and many other great stars. It was non-stop, and Tiny Tim was there as well singing "Tip-toe through the Tulips". The teenagers were swaying to the music and thoroughly enjoying it. We all kept together, we had taken sandwiches and coke, and there were chip vans all over the place.

I started dancing away to Tiny Tim's music and singing, much to the amusement of John, Angela, Catherine and Denise. We had some fellow near us, with a cowboy hat on, and from what I can remember, he had an American accent and I think I was the only one of my age group in that area of the ground. This guy got talking to Angela and asked her "who is that fellow keeping time and enjoying himself? Angela retorted "that is my father", and he shouted out in his American accent "By golly Angela, but you have a groovy Pa". This remark brought great laughter all around, and I felt like a teenager myself. I got immediate acceptance, such was the good mood of everybody. There was a huge attendance at the festival, at least one hundred thousand, the papers next day reported that there were more people at it, than the whole population of the Isle of Wight put together, of course they had swarmed over from the mainland. The concert went on from the Saturday evening right through to the early hours of Sunday morning, youngsters sleeping in the open and in tents round the site. There was a marquee put up on the site and our own Parish Priest, along with several other Priests used it as a chapel to celebrate mass for the large crowds that were there. We ourselves went home, but did not have many hours in bed, as we got up and went to Mass in Shanklin the next morning, we were tired but had thoroughly enjoyed the experience of the previous night.

Eileen as Maid of Honour Shanklin Carnival (top centre)

CHAPTER XIX

Sarah now started school at Ventnor along with Simon and Elizabeth went to Ryde Convent with Angela and Eileen.

In the meantime, I had met an old friend who was with me in former years in Broomfield Hospital while he was doing his training as a male nurse. He was Jack Butler, and I have mentioned him in the earlier part of this book. Well Jack became charge nurse on St. Catherine's Ward during the day, while I was on duty during the night. Jack had finished his training and had been to Whipp's Cross near London. He was very efficient at his work, and still retained his great sense of humour that he had, when we were together in Broomfield in Essex. Jack and I had a great chat on our first meeting as we had been apart such a long time. He had his sorrows, and I had mine, but time is a great healer, and our friendship blossomed forth and the last time I heard, Jack was talking about going on to be a tutor, but someone told me that he is now on the District Nursing. He is a marvellous nurse and gives great confidence to those about him. It was great to meet him in the morning to give him the report from when I took over at night, there was a great bond of friendship over those years and his advice was always welcome. Although Jack was of the Church of England faith, he had a great liking for the dignity of the patient and to see that the Catholic Priests were called, when they were needed for those who wanted to make their peace with God.

Mrs Groves was my nursing officer in charge and Mr. Townsend was second in command on night duty and when Mrs Groves, Mr Townsend and I were on duty together, we shared many happy hours and many heavy nights, when staff were short. They were both very experienced and wonderful to work with, they were very human in their approach and witty with it.

During these years of night work, I had many stomach bleeds, because my doctor had discovered that I had a hiatus hernia. This meant that I found lifting extremely heavy for me, and I had to be on regular courses of antibiotics for my chest. We all worked as a team, and it was nice to have someone to share our problems with. I am sure Mary Groves and George Townsend, must be retired by now, or coming up for it, I do hope Mary if you read this book or it comes your way, that you will be sitting back with your feet up, enjoying your rest. God Bless you and George for making my last years at St. Mary's a time to laugh and recall our many experiences and the funny things that happened in the course of our nursing duties.

While there were plenty of things happening at work, there were often unforgettable things happening at home too.

One evening at the end of the season, a young lad of about fourteen arrived on the doorstep and asked Elsie if she did Bed and Breakfast. She was suspicious, as he was in school uniform and had no luggage. She asked him if he was on his own, she invited him in, because she was worried about him. She told him that he might stay and he signed the visitors book with his full name and address.

Our own children were out, or at least the older ones were, and were due home on the train at any minute, so there was a meal prepared and the table was already set and a plate of buns was in place ready. Elsie asked the lad if he would like a cup of tea and he sat down to drink it. She noticed the buns disappearing one by one and realised he was famished. The children arrived, so she settled him in with them round the table and while they were all eating, she slipped out of the front door and round to the Presbytery a couple of doors away to find Fr. Murray and get his advice. Elsie knew that Fr. Murray had an arrangement with the police to help people in trouble, if they were willing to tell the police the same story as they had told him, he would help them, usually with finances to get home. Elsie came back indoors and Fr. Murray took it from there and informed the police. In the meantime Elsie gave the lad a pair of our son's pyjamas, and settled him down in a small bedroom at the front of the house. He was a lovely boy, well dressed and neat and tidy and extremely polite.

Later that night a plain clothes policeman came round to the house to question him. The police had already contacted the police in the lads area in London, and found that his parents had already reported him missing. Arrangements had been made for his parents to travel to the Island to collect him the next day, they were nice people from London, but it was not the first time their son had disappeared on an adventure. The policeman took the lad away to the police station for the night, although we wanted to keep him and let him have a good rest. It was probably safer that way because he might have absconded during the night and gone off on further adventures. I'd love to know what happened to him, maybe he joined the navy or went to see the world.

Another story was when we had another visitor, shabbily dressed and carrying an "hold-all", land on the doorstep after dark one Sunday night. He looked like someone who had been fishing. He had a very cultured Oxford accent, and it being the end of the season and vacant beds in the house, Elsie invited him in. It was only when he was inside the door, that she realised that he was rather ragged and had no possessions with him except the "hold-all" and an old fashioned gramaphone.

Elsie asked him if he wanted accommodation for the one night, and he replied that he would like to stay for the week. Elsie phoned me up on the ward as I was on duty that night. She sounded rather worried, so I told her to give him a bed just for the one night. Next morning she gave him breakfast in his room, which delighted him, but it was really so that he would not embarrass two teachers from Spain, who were staying with us.

When I arrived home, I found him still there, Elsie having gone out to work herself. Elsie's mother, who was staying with us, was up the wall, and she said "I don't know whatever has come over my daughter, she is allowing that man to stay for a week, and she'll never get paid". I was a bit mad myself about it, but then I was about to go to bed myself, when I saw him on the stairs, and he spoke to me and said what a lovely morning it was, and how kind my wife had been to him. He also told me that he loved music, and that he had his own gramaphone with him and that his sister was a music teacher in a big school. "Well" I said "You will not be able to play your gramaphone indoors here during the day, because I have to sleep because I am on night duty, but you can play it outdoors if you like". Anyhow, as it turned out, he was a proper gentleman, well educated, and a good conversationalist.

When the end of the week came, he was there to pay for his accommodation and was very grateful for everything. It was only afterwards that Elsie told me, that because she had felt sorry for him, she had given him such a huge breakfast, that he was able to pack some of it, and take it out with him, probably down to the beach. He had apparently been working in the public gardens in Ventnor during the season, and we found out later that he was really of aristocratic descent.

On another occasion, Elsie had taken the children to Ryde for music exams, and when they were returning on the train, they noticed a young couple with a baby in a pram. It was pouring with rain when they reached the railway station, so they rushed down the road home, thinking no more about it. Some time later the same couple came to the door with a piece of paper with our address written on it, which someone had given them when they directed them to us for accommodation. Elsie as usual took pity on them, and took them in.

When I came home, I was suspicious, because I had been approached at work to see if we could accommodate a young mother and baby. The Lady Almoner at the hospital had written to me, as of course most people in the hospital knew that I was in the "Life" group for the Isle of Wight, which is the equivalent of Cura in Ireland. At the time I was away from work, and had not received the letter until my return by which time she had been accommodated elsewhere.

I found the chap himself very friendly, and sitting down in our kitchen. Normally we discouraged this, having visitors in the sitting room which was provided for them. The girl was a nice person, and the baby beautiful, and Elsie took over looking after the baby when needed. We provided the couple with their meals, and the girl got herself a job doing a paper round. Although the chap was nice, I thought he was over friendly to my daughter Angela and I was rather uneasy with the situation. A couple of nights later, we attended Evening Devotions in the church in Newport where Elsie played the organ for the special Novena to Our Lady. The family went every Thursday and we would have the Rosary, and a special sermon from Fr Laverty, who was the curate and the chaplain to the prisons. This particular night his sermon was all about helping people, and trusting people, and looking for the best in people. Elsie and myself had been previously discussing the situation that we had at home, I was still suspicious of the set up, and didn't believe that the couple were husband and wife, but I waited for events to happen. On the way home, we discussed what the Priest had been talking about and Elsie would not see eye to eye with me, she was quoting "whatever you do to these little ones, you do unto me". It was rather foggy, and I was so keen on putting over my point of view that on a bend in the road I nearly went into the ditch. On reaching home we found Angela who hadn't been with us, sitting on the floor with the chap who was staying with us, chatting away. I signalled for Angela to go to bed, so that I could get a chance to talk to him by himself. He told me that he had been in the army and that he had been waiting to get into the prison service. He had done his two years National Service which young lads had to do in England after the war. We kept them all that week, and in the meantime I made some enquiries and I found that the girl and the baby had been linked with the Social Services. I came home from work just as Elsie had cooked breakfast for him one morning. The girl was out doing her paper round and he was about to sit down at the table. I asked him to tell me the truth. I told him, he was getting no breakfast, until he became honest with me. He was not the girl's husband, whether he was the father of the baby I do not know, but he admitted that they were not married, and while I was talking to him, the lady from the Social Services called to our front door, and asked about the girl, so I was able to leave everything in their hands, and the couple left us. Apparently they had stayed in other houses on the Island, staying a few days, paying nothing and then on the excuse of going to the laundrette, go out with a blue laundry bag and never return. Some weeks later, there was an article in the paper saying they had been arrested for larceny and fraud, so ended another chapter in our lives.

We had another lady who people called "The Little Flower" like St Thérese of Lisieux. She was a very holy person who was working in a local boarding school at the time, and she would spend the school holidays with us. Later she went to the mainland, but would still come back to us for holidays. She would spend hours praying in the back of the church and you wouldn't see her in the dim light of evening, and she sometimes almost got locked in, when the church was closed for the night. I was rather worried about her because she was not taking food, and I was of the opinion that she was having problems mentally and needed medical help. I tried to reason with her on several occasions but she seemed to be denying herself all but the bare necessities of life. It came out in conversation that she had been married and had a son, now grown up, who had been taken into care by his grandparents while she was suffering from post-natal depression, and she missed him a lot, but followed his progress diligently. The last time she arrived at the door, we were not able to take her in as we were making arrangements at that time to return back to Ireland. We got her sleeping accommodation in another guest house nearby and she came to us for her meals. One morning we had an urgent message to say that she had a stroke and died. Of course no one really knew who she was, or where she came from, but she had told us about her war time experiences in the fire service and the locality, and as she had an uncommon name Elsie tried ringing all the people by that name in the phone directory to try and find her family. God must have been looking after her for the first phone call found her husband, who came and looked after everything, and she was laid to rest on the Island.

I felt that Our Lady was guiding people to us who were having troubles either mentally or physically. We had a couple who used to spend summer holdiays with us, also Easter and Christmas. The wife had been ill and suffered brain damage and it was difficult for her to stay in a hotel, so her husband was delighted when they were guided to us by the Knights of St. Columba. They were lovely people and we had many enjoyable times with them, but the last time they came the wife was very difficult to manage and the husband was poorly too. Our children were growing up fast and had a lot of study to do and the presence of such people, was upsetting them, although they tried hard to understand. We tried to explain to the husband that we might not be able to have them at Christmas this time, but we heard that they both died before they had a chance to return and we felt very sad about it, may the lord have mercy on them!

I tried to help others in need, as best I could, and it was very rewarding. I had the help of the Knights on another occasion to get a poor man who was a brother Knight assistance. He had lost his wife, and had an adult handicapped son. We got him into a private nursing home and the Knights paid for his accommodation, as he was too sick to stay in our house. The social services when they were contacted, managed to find him a place in a branch of St Mary's Hospital at Fairlee Hospital for terminal care and he too passed on. So it was, that even though I had given my life to nursing as my profession, I wasn't able at this time to help by nursing but I was able to arrange that through the organisation of the Knights, we were able to visit him and keep in touch and support him in his last days. This is what fraternity means to us who join that Order.

While I am on the subject of charitable works, I was elected Grand Knight of the Isle of Wight Council in 1971-1972 and I took on a great responsibility because our membership had fallen to thirty-three members, some had left through illness, and some had passed away. The Sunday evening that I was elected, Elsie was admitted to hospital for an operation, and I had the good wishes and prayers of Chaplain and brothers of our Council. Being Grand Knight was a great challenge to me because I had been Social Secretary, Action Convenor for the previous years. We had arranged dinners and dances for the Knights, and Denis Sullivan who was my secretary, and I and the new Social Secretary had to continue doing this. The dances were usually held in the "Oasis Ballroom" in Ryde or the Grantham Hotel in Cowes or any place that the Knights decided upon, but usually it was the "Oasis" in Ryde which has many happy memories for me. We had no problem in selling tickets because it was the highlight of all the other dances and was very popular. We invited all the clergy, the heads of all the other organisations like the Catenians, the Legion of Mary, St Vincent de Paul and in my years as Grand Knight, the Rotarians. All the eight parishes on the Island were represented. The

Opening of St Thomas of Canterbury School in Newport

Knights had all their quarterly Masses in rotation in the different churches round the Island, our work helping the Priests of the Island was well known as we gave them our full loyalty and support. We organised the annual Corpus Christi procession, at the First Holy Communions of the children, the Knights were there giving a helping hand, and also at the Confirmations. During my two years as Grand Knight we increased our members from thirty-three to fifty-five Knights. I had a wonderful team of officers, two of these had been Mayors of Newport, carrying the banner for four years between them. Our Council raised £95,000 for the Catholic schools through the running of football pools, whist drives, beetle drives, jumble sales, cheese and wine parties, coffee mornings etc. Apart from this, we were able to give donations to St Mary's Hospital, the Cheshire Home in Shanklin, while the Youth Club in Shanklin, washed, cleaned and helped prepare the building for the incoming residents of the Cheshire Home. This was arranged by our Youth Officer who was brilliant in keeping the young people away from the drug scene, he arranged lectures for the Youth Club by specialists in that field. My gratitude must go out to the wives of the Knights, who did so much behind the scenes and the Catholic Women's League who under Mrs Joan Coueslant and her successors supported us in our projects — they were great in their generosity. I felt that at last I had reached my life's ambition of being able to lead the Knights in our parishes to the fulfilment that they as Knights might obtain through helping in their areas. They had plenty to get their teeth into, and action not words was their motto.

Happy as we were in our activities, sometimes we would take time off to just relax and enjoy ourselves. Such a time as this was when we chartered a boat for the evening. It picked up Brothers from Bournemouth and Southampton, Gosport, Portsmouth and then made its way across the Solent to Cowes where we went aboard. The greeting when we embarked was enormous and it only seemed a very short time until we landed back at Cowes again after cruising round the Coast of the Isle of Wight. All was gaiety on board. There was a great attendance of knights, their families and friends and everyone was catered for. There was a disco on one deck, a more formal dance on another with a band and tombola and another entertainment on another deck. There was a bar and plenty of food. Everyone had a great time, the atmosphere was so much better than any social on dry land. Of course we were blessed with a very calm sea, it otherwise might not have been quite the same. As it was, it was one of the best nights out we every had.

CHAPTER XX

The Island Churches, Church of England, Baptist and Methodist came together in groups during Lent, in discussion in their homes, and the work of Vatican II and the ideals they expressed were brought to the fore, in a work of love that was steered through by his Lordship Bishop Worlock, now Archbishop of Liverpool. He asked for support through the Parish Councils and through the organisations he set up in the Diocese of Portsmouth. We were in the lead in the South of England, the Channel Islands and to every corner of that Diocese.

We celebrated our 25th Anniversary of the Island Knights by having Mass first in Ryde Parish Church. Bishop Worlock was the main celebrant and the Chaplain of the Order and the other Parish Priests from all the Parishes on the Island were present. The Mass was followed by a dinner-dance and we had great celebrations. I was at this time elected District Deputy for Gosport Council, Portsmouth Council and the Isle of Wight and I was directly responsible for these three Councils to the Provincial Grand Knight. Memories of these years will always be foremost in my heart.

I worked together with the Rotarians on collecting medical drugs that were given as samples to the doctors, through the cooperation of the Island doctors and a pharmacist on the mainland who was one of our members. We were able to help the "War On Want" in the third world countries abroad, and I was informed that we had paid for and sent £70,000 worth of these drugs in the course of a few years. Our thanks must certainly go to Brother Tony O'Donnell, the Provincial Action Convenor from Southampton, and to his fellow brothers who worked so hard during these wonderful years.

For myself I attended the Supreme meeting in Guernsey in 1972 as Grand Knight of Council 411. Elsie came with me, and we were dined and wined by the Grand Knight Brother Joe Stagg and his Council. Different parties of us stayed in the homes of the Knights in Guernsey, and were made to feel a real part of the family and community and were shown all the intricasies of how to grow tomatoes, and other facets of their island life. Brother Michael May was the Supreme Knight, and with him we attended a champagne party as guests of the Island Parliament and the ladies as well as their husbands were really merry by the time lunch was served, no glass was ever left to get empty and while the conversation was in full swing, no one noticed how many refills had been acquired. The ladies were entertained, being given a conducted tour of the Island while the Knights held a meeting for all the Officers and Brothers of the Province. I remember well that Brother May said "Good afternoon, Brothers and fellow alcoholics". Most of the resolutions were adopted as some of the Brothers were almost ready to nod off during the course of the meeting. The banquet which was part of the weekend was fantastic. There was so much choice of food, all beautifully prepared, and we were looked after so well.

During the banquet Guernsey's Bailiff, Sir William Arnold told a gathering of Roman Catholics at the Duke of Richmond Hotel "God doesn't live in a luxury flat in Heaven, he is on earth with us all". He was proposing the toast of the Order of the Knights of St Columba and their guests. "About once a year for a great many years I have seen in the local newspaper, a photo of a few stalwart gentlemen, with mysterious titles and imposing regalia. Apart from reading that they were Knights of St Columba I confess this was one of the many things about which I know very little." In proposing the toast to the Order said Sir William "I feel like the newly appointed Parish Priest who was being shown round the church by a faithful member of the Order who said—"You will have to speak up here Father, the agnostics in here are terrible."

Sir William had heard how the local Councils had sponsored the mentally handicapped children on the Faith and Light pilgrimage to Lourdes. Unity, charity and fraternity are the virtues the Knights try to live up to. Sir William remembered one of them which was Charity—often interpreted as putting your hand in your pocket—or better still, squeezing a donation out of someone else!—but he said charity was one of the greatest words in the English language. Its simplicity denotes sincerity—its implication is service before self and not merely the giving of a donation. Praising the work of the Order again Sir William said "this Order, which I salute this evening for its splendid contribution to the well being of our people, is one I commend to the attention of everybody in this Island". Brother Michael May paid tribute to the Clergy on the Island, and he praised the work of Brother Joe Stagg and the fast growing Guernsey Council.

Next day as we flew out from Guernsey Airport back to Southampton, we were treated like royalty, everyone was there to wave us off, and we were sorry to be leaving such a wonderful people so soon. Flying over the Isle of Wight on our way home, we were asked by Brother Michael May to organise a quarterly meeting on the Island "Brother Simon—it is over to you" he said, and so with Brother Denis Sullivan my secretary, plans were started on board that plane that Sunday afternoon and the meeting was arranged to take place in October 1972 at Newport the capital of the Isle of Wight. This was the first time in the history of the Island Council that anything so big Elsie and her colleagues arranged a buffet luncheon in the Church hall, and everything went off well.

Another project of the Knights was to help with Prison Visitation. I was for three years attending Albany Prison every Saturday morning as a Catechist in conjunction with Sr Cecilia Kavanagh, the sister of the famous Irish poet Patrick Kavanagh who was a sister of the Presentation order in Ryde, and with Mr William Rogers, a school master. We would spend about three hours which included Rosary and Benediction for the inmates. Discussions were organised by the prisoners themselves and chaired by all three people under the guidance of the prison chaplain Fr. Laverty. We used to have a cup of tea accompanied by cakes provided by Nuns and Mr Rogers and myself supplied

J

Children from Northern Ireland on holiday on the Isle of Wight. Above: a picnic at Alum Bay.

cigarettes or tobacco for those who preferred to roll their own cigarettes. It was a refreshing three hours, and a Catholic action that is to be encouraged with no political strings attached. These sessions were very much appreciated by the prisoners, and they looked forward to them, as it fulfilled a gap in their lives where frustration must enter from time to time.

In July 1972, the Supreme Knight had arranged that the Knights of St Columba would be responsible for bringing three hundred and sixty children from both Catholic and Protestant families from war torn Northern Ireland to have holidays in England and Wales with host families who were to be distributed throughout the different provinces. Each area arranged for the children of both denominations to be in close proximity to each other, during that period. It was my pleasure on the Monday morning to meet my brother Knights in Southampton and bring four children to the Isle of Wight. Two girls stayed with us in Atherley Road and the two boys stayed with Lloyd Bunce and his wife near Sandown. I had finished my duties at the hospital having worked all Sunday night and I caught the Red Funnel steamer from West Cowes and met the four children in Southampton. Ten other children went to the Portsmouth area, more to the New Forest and Bournemouth. I took our four home in a raging thunderstorm, so it was an eventful trip.

We had a sale of work outside the Church in Shanklin by kind permission of Father Henry Donnelly, people were very generous, and it was decided that the proceeds would be used to bring the children from the province over for a day's outing and tour of the Isle of Wight. My own children joined in, and several reports in the local press did great justice to the venture. I have some photographs taken at Alum Bay where we all had a picnic on the beach. The Sisters of Mercy in Shanklin invited them back to the Convent for high tea. We took the children who stayed with us to join in the activities in the youth clubs around the Island, and by the end of the holiday, the children were smiling, happy and contented.

I must thank all my numerous benefactors who supplied ice cream and money to make their outing and whole holiday, a beautiful memory that will remain with them for many years to come. I want to thank all my fellow parishioners, Father Henry Donnelly, now retired and the Mercy Sisters in the Convent in Shanklin.

The two boys, on the boat coming over, were very shy and I had to carry the conversation between them and the two girls. After the holiday was over, on the return boat journey to Southampton, I went down to the lower deck, all four were laughing and starry eyed and relaxed completely enjoying their own company. What a contrast to the first meeting I had with them, so it goes to prove that if peace could reign in the hearts of both communities and take example from these four children which I had the pleasure of meeting in 1972, how different would our world be generally. Please God I hope that our prayers at Fatima, Medjugorje, will be answered and that Our Lady Queen of Peace will bring the peace which is so badly needed in this our land.

Mother Veronica and Fr. Richier on our Pilgrimage to Lisieux

Feast of the Assumption August 15th in Lisieux

CHAPTER XXI

The next summer Elsie and I together with our daughter Eileen went on a pilgrimage to Lisieux for the centenary celebrations of St. Thérèse. We went with a group from the Isle of Wight. Father Richer from Newport was our chaplain, and altogether they were a great crowd. We travelled by ferry from Southampton to Cherbourg on 13th August having a marvellous crossing, the weather being hot and calm. From Cherbourg we travelled to Lisieux by coach enabling us to see much of the lovely Normandy countryside, large fields divided into strips, cows being milked in the open, and quaint old fashioned villages. The hostel where we stayed was built round a quadrangle and each floor was identical, sometimes causing much confusion especially when ones key happened to fit another door. It being very hot weather, all the windows were open, and one morning we awoke to the sounds of the boy choristers — who were housed across the quadrangle opposite our room — having a great pillow fight, there were screams and shouts of laughter. Later we saw them processing up the aisle of the Basilica looking just like perfect angels.

The room where we ate was very basic with scrubbed wooden tables and real French food served — a bowl of cocoa for breakfast, delicious croissants, plenty of fresh fruit, wine at every meal, served in big jugs and delicious fromage frais. After the evening meal we would use the same room for our discussions after the days outings. One night we sat there, when Mother Veronica, an elderly sister who made the pilgrimage with us, suddenly jumped up and started shaking her long skirts. As she did so, out ran a little mouse. Luckily she was not a bit perturbed and after all the laughter had subsided we were able to carry on with the serious side of the talks. Mass was said each day in the little chapel and Elsie was called upon to play the hymns on the very old harmonium. The days went very quickly, we visited all the places connected with St Thérèse — her home, her convent, the church where she prayed and other places of interest. One of these was a hospital, where the sisters had in their care, the vestments actually worn by St Thomas of Canterbury, when he was assassinated in Canterbury Cathedral. There was a long story of how they actually came to be in the possession of the nuns, but there they were, preserved in a large suitcase and we were actually able to touch them and put religious objects like rosary beads, to touch them. We were told that we were very privileged and might be the last group able to do so, as the vestments were to be put in a sealed glass case.

The highlight of the pilgrimage was August 15th of course and there was a huge procession round the outside of the Basilica with a wonderful Mass inside, a day never to be forgotten. Before leaving France we were fortunate in being able to visit the Cathedral of Bayeux and across the road from the Cathedral the much celebrated Bayeux tapestries.

It was hard to break away from Lisieux and return home, not only had we a wonderful pilgrimage with all the religious exercises and the chance to learn so much about St Thérèse and her life, but also we had made friends with the people of the town. When the coach pulled away up the street from the hostel on its homeward journey to Le Havre, people were out on the street waving us goodbye and cheering us on our way, the crowd included the lady from the tavern where with much sign language we made them understand we desired to partake of lager and also maybe the gentleman from the supermarket, where one morning about nine o'clock I tried out my best French, greeting the mirth stricken man with "Bon soir Monsieur".

It was during this period of time that Aunt Maud became very ill and I paid her a visit and she wanted me to stay with her. She had failed a lot and I did not want to leave her alone, but then again I was living miles away with a wife and family to care for, but I kept in touch by phone, and I thought I might be able to transfer her to a hospital near us, but with her independent spirit, she would not agree to that. I also kept in touch with the Parish Priest in that area, and he visited her regularly, then one weekend I rang her, and she seemed very distressed so I got in touch with the Social Services who were very helpful and eventually got her admitted to the hospital where she had been a pharmacist. I visited Aunt Maud and had the pleasure of meeting her godson and his wife and they visited her frequently and kept in touch with me. I was on duty one night in February when I got a call to say that Aunt Maud had passed away, R.I.P., so I got a few days compassionate leave, and Elsie and myself made all the arrangements in England, and I got in touch with Fr John who made the necessary arrangements in Ireland where she was to be brought for burial. I flew home with her remains to Cork airport.

I remember saying to the lady next to me on the plane, when she asked if I was coming home on holiday, that I was returning on a sad occasion, and that my Aunt's coffin was on our plane, I never saw anyone disappear so quickly when we landed at Cork airport. Aunt Maud was brought to Rossmore Church in West Cork, arriving around 9 p.m., and it amazed me to see the crowds there, patiently awaiting the arrival, and they all spoke about her, although she had been so long away. It was a reuniting of all the members of the family but Aunt Kathleen her sister was not able to be present, as she herself was elderly and indisposed. Fr John offered up the Requiem Mass for the repose of her soul and Fr Casey who had known Aunt Maud in England came across to the graveside to offer his condolences.

It was lovely meeting my young cousin Josephine again, and I spent about a week in Cork on this occasion. Josephine showed me around most of Cork city and her friends in Kinsale were extremely kind to me. Her mother Muriel took me out to lunch, and we had a great chat about old times and she looked very smart as usual. I paid a few visits to my friends in Ballygurteen, but then I began to not feel too well and was to learn that I had developed mumps. Luckily for me I was staying in O'Donovan's Hotel in Clonakilty which was run by a wonderful lady. She nursed me and looked after me, brought me hot water bottles and lovely dishes of soup which I was able to swallow and looked after me like a mother until I was fit enough to attempt the journey home, which luckily didn't take too long by air, and I was able to recuperate at home before tackling the job of sorting out all Aunt Maud's affairs, which fell to me, being the only member of the family in England.

At this time I was in constant touch with the family in Ireland and that, together with all the friendship shown me on my recent visit, gave me the feeling that I would like to return to West Cork and I began to give it serious thought.

I knew at this time that I was having more stomach bleeds, and living on antibiotics in the winter months and taking more time off from work and it was possible that I might have to give up working altogether. If this came about, I knew now, where I would settle.

In the meantime I carried on with the nursing to the best of my ability. The hospital staff knew that I was a Knight of St Columba and one time, one of our brothers was sick in the acute ward of St Mary's Hospital. He was taken very ill and we had on our ward, a phone call from the "top hospital" to send up the Grand Knight.

Our charge nurse Mr Townsend who was in charge that night came rushing into my ward, with a huge grin on his face, and he said "are you a Grand Knight?" When I said "yes", he said "where have you left your horse? and where is your sword? — You are urgently wanted at the top hospital — would you like a lift up sir?". This patient had a slight heart attack and he wanted me to contact the Catholic Priest, and then he wanted me to bring his wife from home which I did for him. He lived a few years after that, but I shall always remember how Mr Townsend took advantage of that situation and brought great laughter among all the nursing staff.

I remember on another occasion, a patient who was terribly well educated, who had a terminal disease, as he said "goodnight" to me, he seemed so peaceful and resigned in his way of acceptance. When I took his temperature in the morning, he looked up to me, and he said "what a pleasure it is, to wake up, and see such a lovely day, and your smiling face to greet in this day" and his features portrayed that inner happiness that shines through, that God had spared him for another day. Even now, as I look back over those years of nursing, the compliment that patient paid me that morning will always remain in my heart, as in gratitude for being part of that happiness. I think the song of today "One Day At a Time Sweet Jesus" just about sums it all up. There have been mornings in my life since when I remember what he said.

It was at the Knights of St Columba Silver Jubilee Dinner that I appealed for people to attend the Abortion Rally in Hyde Park in London on Sunday April 28th 1974. 85,000 people paraded that day in a procession, eight deep. They did so with dignity and marked silence. We had a nice crowd from the Island and we arranged two coaches in Portsmouth to take us to the rally. I had a small placard with "Isle of Wight group" written on it. Many nuns from the

Isle of Wight Group at the Abortion Rally

Island were with us and as I came across off the boat at Portsmouth somebody said to me "what group are you?" The nuns burst out laughing when I replied that we were the Singing Nun's group.

When we were in Hyde Park, from across the large platform for the public speakers, a photographer zoomed one of their special cameras in our direction, and I hoisted my notice higher. Not thinking any more about it, I was at home next morning and Knights from the mainland were phoning me, to say that my photograph was foremost in the "Daily Express", so I went out to get that paper, and there, sure enough was the "Isle of Wight group" placard surrounded by the Rev Mother from Shanklin and all our crowd from the Island as you will see from the photograph which is included.

Another morning, having been on duty all night, I went up to London to meet two members of Parliament, who were supporting the amendment to the Abortion Act. I met Shirley Williams and then I travelled back that evening, just in time to go on duty again that night. Fair play to my sister-in-charge Mary Groves, she let me have a longer break, in order to have a sleep. She said "I am not a Catholic but I support you a hundred per cent for the rights of the unborn child. We had another rally in Southampton, another dignified march organised by the local bodies and the Knights. The opposition approached us, and my daughter Eileen debated the issue with them in an open air park, and they were all debating in a friendly atmosphere.

I must not forget that while we were in Shanklin, Simon received his Confirmation. Bishop Worlock officiated at the Confirmation which was in the evening when the nights were dark early. There was a power cut, and the Church had to be candle lit. When speaking to the boys and girls the Bishop made some remark about the Holy Ghost not being in favour or some such remark. Later on the Bishop announced about letting there be light. At the same instant, the church became ablaze with light as the electrical current was restored. It was just like a miracle.

Sarah received her First Communion in Shanklin Church and that year a great Corpus Christi Procession was held in the grounds of East Cowes Convent. These were very happy moments in our lives, as well as theirs.

I gradually began having to take more time off from work. I had chronic bronchitis, stomach bleeds, tennis elbow, gout and Menieres disease of the ears. I was advised to retire from work in nursing and just try a light seasonable job, which would be easier for me. I was at home several months before I was officially retired in the spring of 1975.

I took up part time work on the counter in the café at Brown's Golf course in Sandown during the day and I worked in the Spa Bar on Shanklin front at night where I worked for an Irish man named Noel. I did the washing up of glasses and took over the sausage roll and snack counter. "The Three Pennies" were the group that were playing there for two or three seasons and I used to lead Kathy the lead vocalist on to the dance floor, and this encouraged other couples on to the floor, and then Kathy would say, now the handsome Irishman with the green bow-tie can go back to his sausage rolls. Elsie used to come down before the end of the evening and we would have an hour dancing together while the older children baby-sat. We used to walk home arm in arm tired but happy — not having to do night work any more was a great relief.

I thought a great deal about the future and what would be the best thing to do. I gradually made up my mind, and one day when Elsie came in from work, I greeted her with "we are going back to Ireland to live". She was quite stunned but realised that was what I would like, so we agreed and started to make enquiries about the possibilities, and started writing off for information about houses that were advertised for sale. As the weeks passed our plans for selling our house in Shanklin gained momentum, and so it was that in May 1975, I took Elsie and Sarah to West Cork to look for a house, once again staying in O'Donovan's Hotel in Clonakilty.

Mrs Matt O'Sullivan was very helpful and took us around to look at different houses while Matt was away in Dublin. Anyhow on his return Matt took us to see a cottage on half an acre of ground just outside Clonakilty on the Dunmanway road. A small shop was established there, selling minerals, ice cream, cigarettes, bread, milk and other essential groceries. We fell in love with the place and Bill and Rose Santry were a lovely friendly couple and Matt and myself soon struck the bargain. The next day Bill and Rose took us round the local country side by car and on a visit to Aunt Kathleen who only lived three miles away.

We went to the Convent in Clonakilty to make arrangements for Sarah's schooling and to the local Vocational school to make arrangements for Simon as it was nearby. However when Simon came he opted to travel to Skibbereen to attend St Fachtna's de la Salle School as he had been attending the De la Salle College in Southsea which he liked very much.

We returned home to the Isle of Wight travelling on the "Innisfallen" from Cork to Swansea, a boat that was to have many happy memories for Elsie and myself in the years ahead.

We started to make our plans, Elsie finished working in school meals in October when the schools started the half-term holidays, we managed to sell our house and we booked to move at the end of October.

At this time John had had his 21st Birthday and was established in the Civil Service in Croydon, Angela was doing her BA in Fine Art in Norwich, Eileen was doing teacher training in Southampton, Elizabeth was settled in a job in the Bank and didn't wish to leave the Island, we arranged accommodation for her, wishing that she might change her mind and follow us, while Simon and Sarah were still at school, and naturally came with us.

The time for leaving soon came and it was with very mixed feelings that we said our Goodbyes. We had really enjoyed living on the Island and had made so many friends. The last Sunday that we were there, we went round to make the coffee and tea after Mass in the Church Hall. We were taken by surprise as a presentation had been arranged. The parishioners gave us a lovely clock. I was so overcome I just burst into tears and couldn't speak. "Well" said Fr. Donnelly "That is the first time I have ever seen Simon stuck for words!"

The Knights of St Columba Isle of Wight Silver Jubilee

Bishop Worlock

CHAPTER XXII

We wondered how life in Ireland would compare with the Isle of Wight, how we would feel leaving the family behind and many other things, but soon the day for us to move house arrived — everything was packed except for a few things which we would need after the removal van had gone. Early in the morning, the van arrived, our furniture was packed and went off to catch the ferry on its start for the long journey to West Cork. We ourselves had another couple of days to wait before going, sleeping in sleeping bags in an empty house and being able to cook a meal in the Church Hall next door, the time passed quickly. Our turn came and there we were, with our little yellow Reliant three wheeler packed to overflowing with a full roof rack on top. These were the "few necessary things" which we had held back from the removal van. How on earth Elsie, Simon and Sarah were able to find room for themselves amongst it all, remains a mystery. The neighbours gave us a great cheer as we started off on our journey. All went well until we reached Swansea. There we were met by the news that the boat to Ireland had been cancelled and there we were stranded, our furniture by now in Ireland and us still in England. We had planned to arrive at our new home at the same time as the furniture which had three other deliveries to make to different parts of Ireland before unloading our furniture. We tried to get in touch with the solicitor in Ireland but all the telephone lines were down near Clonakilty due to storms and floods. We stayed in a guest house on the sea front at the Mumbles and actually had a relaxing two days, hoping that all would be well in Ireland.

When we arrived in Clonakilty it was Halloween. Our furniture had arrived and most of it was taken indoors by the previous owners, but more had to be left in the garage. Tired out, we slept well that night, little worried by spirits or witches or any other such phenomena. The next morning "All Saints" we went to Mass, all the shops were closed it being a Feast Day, we managed to get a food shop open. We were desperate to get an electric plug as ours did not fit the sockets, so when we were directed to a lady in an electrical shop. We were overjoyed when she took us in and provided what was wanted. We felt that life was going to be good. We soon settled down to our little cottage and the shop was a great idea for getting to know our neighbours and making friends. I visited my old friends in Ballygurteen and Rossmore and people who went to school with me.

My first idea was to enlarge the shop and put an extension on to the cottage for this purpose, as the present shop was in the one time "parlour", and I wanted to return the cottage to its original use. We put in a new front door using a stained glass window in it, which we had brought with us. The stained glass window was a picture of Our Lady of Lourdes. It was already in the door when we bought the house in Newport and as we had promised, we took it with us. For safety we had put the window wrapped in corrugated cardboard under a bed. Unfortunately the bed was placed under a window and when

Elsie went to open the window, her foot went under the edge of the bed and her foot crushed the glass. It was not possible to match the glass, but the cracks were leaded so that we could place it in the door. With the light shining behind it at night, it shone, and could be seen on the main Clonakilty road.

After a couple of weeks Elsie and myself attended a meeting of teachers and parents in O'Donovan's Hotel. As Sarah was settling in school at Clonakilty Convent, we felt it was only right that we should take an interest at local level. Several subjects were discussed and I spoke on one item, where my experience from the Isle of Wight may have influenced my idea for speaking. I had of course introduced myself to the various people, and I got a friendly greeting from everybody. They were electing officers for the following year and Mr Walsh was elected chairperson for another year, and the post of vice-chairman was not filled. To my amazement I was approached to become vice-chairman, being referred to, as the gentleman who had spoken earlier. So it was, that within a couple of weeks in Clonakilty I was already taking an active role in the community.

Elsie was really enjoying looking after the shop, and we saw a great need for home made cakes, apple tarts, sausage rolls and other baking. We bought a caravan and put it in the garden for when any of our family and friends might come to stay from England. There was to be a coursing match just up the road from us, so we took the caravan up to the gate and with the stove we made hot soup, cups of tea and provided other refreshments from the shop. We served the refreshments out through the windows, like a mobile chip van. It was great fun for us and was appreciated by the crowd on the cold day.

That gave us the idea of opening the shop for teas and snacks as well as groceries. Once we had the extension built on, we started to make progress. My wife never charged too much and we often had visitors from the town who walked out and sat down to a quiet cup of tea and home made cakes. Elsie's name was gaining momentum in the town, and so were her sausage rolls, and apple tarts which became very popular indeed.

The first winter in Ireland over, it was time to pay our first visit to England for our eldest daughters wedding in March. It was a few days before our departure when our son Simon was taken trout fishing by a neighbour. He hadn't been away too long, when he came home holding out two small trout. He was delighted with himself, but he was dripping wet, having in his excitement fallen into the water. He bathed and changed and we didn't think too much about the accident.

Simon never mentioned feeling ill and we all set off in our three wheeler — Elsie, Simon, Sarah and myself. We drove to Rosslare and although the sun was shining and it was warm, Simon was shaking with the cold. As the boat journey progressed he got more and more feverisn and the steward put us in a side room where he could be quiet. When we reached Wales we didn't know whether to find the nearest hospital or to carry on with the journey. However I drove as far as Bristol, where we pulled into a car park and had about two hours sleep before driving on. As soon as we reached the Isle of Wight, we got Simon to bed and called the doctor. He got treatment and forty eight hours almost solid sleep and was recovered in time for the wedding.

My brother Father John performed the wedding ceremony and we had a family Mass that morning. Fr John looked down at us and he said that he thought that it was a funeral he was attending, as Elsie, Angela who was the bride and myself were all crying after his homily. All our friends from Essex were there for the wedding together with the relations and friends from the Island. Angela and her friend who came from college with her to take the photographs stayed at Peter her husband's home, where his mother had been helping Angela make her dress and make the arrangements in our absence. Fr Donnelly put us up in the Parish House which was very helpful.

Fr Donnelly gave a lovely homily during the wedding ceremony in the afternoon. John Garr was playing the organ. As Angela crossed the forecourt from the car on my arm, she seemed very nervous but looked beautiful, Elizabeth and Sarah and her cousin Beverley were bridesmaids. The ceremony went off very well although Fr John had a heavy dose of influenza. We had a lovely buffet reception in an hotel belonging to a friend of the family. We were lucky that we had a lovely day weatherwise, the next day when we drove home there was deep snow and the snow ploughs were out in Wales.

We had gone to England a few days early for the wedding and took with us a large box of Shamrock for St Patrick's Day which was given out at Mass and at the annual St Patrick's Day dance which was held at the Channel View Hotel where we had a great night. We had a great welcome and it was as if we had never left. Also we had a marvellous welcome when we arrived back in Clonakilty. Although tired, we were very happy to be received with open arms when the neighbours came running to see how the wedding went. All this after less than six months in our new home.

We soon settled back, and we were soon invited to join in helping the Cork Polio Association to raise funds. The first two weeks in May every year there is a door to door collection known as "The Flowers of Hope". A packet of flower seeds is given to every home in return for a donation which goes to help the mentally handicapped of the area in providing schools, workshops, hostels and other facilities. The scheme was originally started to help people who had been hit by polio, but now that polio is not so common, it was decided to help other handicapped people. We were shown the different areas and accompanied other collectors for the first two years until we knew our way around and were able to go out on our own. The roads are so numerous in West Cork that it was very difficult to make up ones mind which road to take at the many crossroads, to make it easier to cover the area. One day we managed to call at the same house three times coming at it from different directions each time. Luckily the owner had a good sense of humour. We are slightly better at it these days, but we covered a large area, from our corner of Ballyduvane through to Rossmore, Ballygurteen, and as far as the approaches to Dunmanway and then back over the hills to Carrigfadda and Reenascreena. We made so many friends doing this collection each year, the people looking forward to getting the "Flowers of Hope" and being very generous in their donations.

Mr Birmingham and several of his committee from the Cork Polio Association in Cork used to come to O'Donovan's Hotel in Clonakilty each year when the collection was finished and be presented with a cheque. Other funds were raised with other events, sales of work, fashion shows and such like.

One day I told our treasurer that I had done a "Dick Emery act" in England for charity. She told me that they were planning a fashion show in the Emmet Hotel and asked me would I do the act during the interval. I readily agreed, so I put on my Auntie's old curly wig, and a costume of Elsies, her tights, my patent dancing shoes and dark glasses. There was no changing room so I had no choice but to change in the gents cloakroom, and as I was coming out, a gentleman came in. As he saw me, he went out again, and looked at "Gents" written over the door and he made some remark to the treasurer who was collecting at the door. She was in fits of laughter but the confused man was not amused, he went in to the owner of the hotel, who was serving behind the bar. By this time I too was in the bar selling raffle tickets, and he complained about the woman coming out of the mens toilets. He said "I thought this was a decent hotel — all the times I have stayed here, nothing like this has happened to me!" He turned and saw me, and then he realised that I was someone dressing up, and even bought some raffle tickets from me. I had arranged with the chairman of the committee to come out as I did my act by walking down the cat walk after all the ladies had finished, and with Eslie's handbag I struck him in the chest shouting "You are awful, but I do like you" — Dick Emery's famous catch phrase. It was a wonder I did not knock him out. Elsie was having a hard job not to give the game away as people in the audience were asking her who it was that was dressed up and she was pretending ignorance.

Next day I went down to the bank and asked to see the manager. I asked him for a loan to pay for the extension to the shop. He said "For Dick Emery — anything!" A few nights after that I came out of the Tally-Ho Bar and as I crossed to my three-wheeler, somebody shouted across the street. "Good night Dick".

One episode I wish to recall during the days of the original old shop caused a great laugh. I was out in the garden talking to a gentleman whose daughter thought she had lost her gold watch near our house when her car had hit the bridge which was part of a very bad corner outside our house — he came to see if any one had found it. Sarah came rushing out to us. "Daddy there is a drunken man in the shop, and he has his arms round Mammy" "Good luck to him" says I, and this gentleman looked so surprised at my reply, and it was told in Clonakilty. Poor Elsie managed tactfully to make her escape. To get behind the counter in the shop, one had to pass by the customer, lift the hinged part of the counter and open a small door. It was while she was trying she had been caught, but no harm was intended, all the man wanted was some "Sweet Afton" cigarettes. Memories of these years in Ballyduvane will always be pleasant although my health from time to time was not too good, several stomach bleeds and bronchitis.

CHAPTER XXIII

We attended daily Mass in Clonakilty, and soon I was involved in the Legion of Mary and became a member. Of course I had also been approached by a member of the Knights of St Columbanus to join the local council, which I did shortly after returning to Ireland. I was invited to Skibbereen to give a talk to the brothers about the organisation of the Knights of St Columba in England.

I also became involved in the organisation of The Parents and Friends of the mentally handicapped, which was to compliment the work of Cork Polio also, but this organisation was trying to get a school in Bantry for the local mentally handicapped, so that they would not have to travel such long distances to Cork, and could attend school daily instead of having to be away from home from Monday until Friday. The Association of Parents and Friends provides funds for providing things like buses and other necessities and on a lighter note arranges an annual summer outing, and a Christmas party for the physically and mentally handicapped people, and the Spastic Society. The local committee was organised by Finbarr O'Donovan and other parents, who had children of their own in these categories. To raise funds, concerts were held, also talent contests among other things. Several famous singers from Dublin came, including Anna McGoldrick and Fr Cleary, the Singing Priest who travelled by car from Ballyfermot. They came to Connolly's Hotel at Ownahincha, where a great Sunday night's entertainment was provided. Jackie Kingston our P.R.O. was very successful in this area and great tribute must be paid to him for arranging for big stars to come from all over Ireland to give us support. This was a very active committee. I played Santa Claus on several occasions in Dunmanway at the Parkway Hotel and at Ownahincha and enjoyed every minute. Each member works tremendously hard, and they are a pleasure to work with. They gave Bantry a great help when they first started their group.

Having been a member of both organisations, brings home to each and everyone of us, how fortunate we are to have our faculties, and how much we can learn from the innocence and the happiness that surrounds each and everyone of these children, whose love radiates on their faces, the inward happiness of their souls, and their close proximity to Our Lady and Jesus himself.

I was interviewed by a member of Cork Radio some years ago, when they were invited to come and meet members of the Association of Parents and Friends of the mentally handicapped in Connolly's Hotel. They wanted to know why I was involved. I told them then, and I again say in this book, that I was fortunate to have six lovely children — four girls and two boys — with no mental or physical handicap and that in gratitude to God, for the blessing we had, I felt privileged to be a member of that Association. At last they are getting the recognition that they should have had over the years. We are now thank God, a caring society and the youth of the country are becoming more involved and enjoying mixing with and helping these people. It is a meaningful work, and gives back to these parents, who have endured so much, the dignity that they and their children deserve. Eileen our daughter who teaches these children in the Convent in Bantry and the other teacher who is so terribly dedicated to her class, will tell you how rewarding the work is, and how close these children become to their teachers. The support given by the Sisters in the Convent, the support of the Clergy and the hotels of West Cork who give the facilities of their hotels without charge are to be highly commended. There are many organisations, like the Wheelchair Society, Rehab and so many more, all with one common cause to make the needs of the handicapped known and appreciated and to get things done to help, being it lowering pavements, providing ramps, guide dogs and a hundred and one other things which people do not realise are a problem to some individuals.

John L. O'Sullivan, Jack Lynch, W.T. Cosgrave, Jim O'Keeffe, Joe Walsh, Paddy Sheehan and not forgetting John McCarthy, all the councillors and public representatives are to be highly commended for their full support at all times for the less fortunate in our society.

Organisations from across the water also gave their time and energy to come and attend seminars. I have been to several of these seminars and it is nice to see the two countries having such an understanding. In comparing different bodies whose freedoms we are all fighting for together, why then are there so many bitter comments towards those who are fighting for the protection of the unborn child. Why cannot all Christian organisations, love one another in charity and fraternity and support each other. If we were all sincere in the practice of our Christian beliefs, there should be no need for abortion clinics. If we all support each other in a Christ like way, then those children who have gone astray, should have first of all, the love and support of their parents and then everything else will follow.

There are Life groups in England who give support and counselling to girls who find themselves pregnant, and there are groups like Cura in this country who will give them support. There is St Anne's Adoption Society in Cork and other such groups and advice centres. Details are given in every doctor's surgery and in the backs of our Churches. Where there is genuine sorrow and need for help there are all the facilities in the church to come close to Christ. There is all this love and people with open arms ready to help, so with highly trained confidential people to assist, why not take advantage of it. Things are never as bad as they may seem.

I have tried in this autobiography to portray my work in England and Ireland, not for a halo, or to look for compliments but to show you the way forward in preserving the "Sanctity of Life", as I have been witness to in thirty-eight years of nursing in my own life. I have been through the second world war to fight for the freedom of the Sanctity of Life for others and their right to live in peace and harmony. In all her messages at Fatima and Medugorje to the children and even here in Ireland, Our Lady has asked for prayer and penance, and prayer to protect the youth of Ireland. They are going out from

Our house at Ballyduvane

Ireland, just as I did so many years ago, the pitfalls are even greater now than they were then—the videos with violent overtones, the soap operas, with so much glamour, that the sanctity of marriage and the beauty of that relationship is destroyed through lustful inuendos. There are so many beautiful things in this world that could be concentrated on. The love of music and the arts can give so much happiness we are lucky to have these things encouraged in Ireland. We have our Irish dancing, Tops of the Town. We have our GAA games, we have so many wonderful athletes we have a culture that the rest of Western Europe cannot provide and so much talent. The devil is out there trying to destroy all these innocent pleasures which we have been reared to. There are so many strands in our society that are trying to destroy family life. Even now Mrs Thatcher realises that the Divorce laws are made so easy that no chance is given for support groups and marriage counsellors to be given a chance to operate, that she is hoping to bring in legislation to make divorce less easy to obtain. Unfortunately all these things are becoming apparent in Ireland now. All the things which we came home to get away from, alas have followed us over.

Elsie and myself became involved in the West Cork Tourism Association and attended all the meetings in Clonakilty and did our little bit towards tourism. I built two tables outside on the lawns with large sun umbrellas over each table, and we served teas, minerals and ice creams. The weekends were busy, especially when the children were home from school. Sarah was excellent in the shop and kept it spotless, she really enjoyed it.

We had a notice put up, half way down the road to Clonakilty. Elsie had done a drawing of a teapot, and we called the shop "The Tea Cosy". I supplied the poetry that went with it, something like this

Come and sit awhile and dream
By Ballyduvane's country stream.
Simon

I have seen English cars stop, and people get out and photograph our notice. Of course one morning on my way to 10 o'clock Mass I found it missing. Someone must have thrown it over the ditch. We often had people call for breakfast after coming off the boat in Cork, we were the first eating place that they would find open, there were very few small cafés at that time, now its very easy to find somewhere for a snack.

Inside the shop I had some iron gates made by Tony Murphy in Clonakilty to separate the eating area from the shop area and some high stools to sit up against the counter. The curved iron in the black gates was painted golden. It was all nicely laid out and we had storage heaters to keep the place warm in winter.

We had the Station Mass in the house and we used the shop area. We put away the groceries and put all the chairs on one side of the gates and set up the

Altar on the other side of the gate and Monsignor Barrett R.I.P. was very impressed by it. "Simon" he said "It is like your own private oratory". It was wonderful to have the privilege of having Mass said in the house and all the neighbours there. As well as being a Station it was like a coming home party and we chatted on until the early hours of the morning.

Another time that we had Mass in the same place, was on the occasion of our Silver Wedding Anniversary in 1978. Most of the family were present at it. Fr John celebrated the special Mass and during the Mass Elsie and I renewed our wedding vows using the same books that Fr John had given to us twenty-five years earlier when he had celebrated the Wedding Mass. My brothers and sisters came from Longford for the occasion and we also invited friends and neighbours. John Joe Hicks brought along his accordian, which he and Fr John took turns at playing and Fr John played the spoons. We had a great night with singing and dancing. We had some beautiful presents and cards given to us. We thank God for having twenty-five good years to be able to celebrate.

Elsie and I have renewed our marriage vows on several occasions since — once in the Convent in Ballyphehane in Cork where Fr McAuliffe celebrated the Mass, and on our 35th Anniversary we had the privilege of sharing in the Community Mass in Myross Wood, the local Retreat Centre, and renewing our vows which Fr Clarkson had specially prepared for us, and to whom I shall indeed be grateful.

On this occasion I made a tape of the different readings I have done in Church on different occasions, both in Clonakilty at reconciliation services organised by Monsignor Daly and again at St Peter's Carrigfadda. I included my favourite prayers taken from the Knock Prayer book which concludes with a prayer for a husband and wife where both our voices are recorded, also different psalms I had read for Fr McAuliffe on the occasion of the Community Hall opening in Reenascreena. I finished the tape with a beautiful recording called "Sailing By" which is the lovely tune which closes the programme on BBC Radio 4 at half past midnight every night — it always reminds me of the boats sailing by in the Isle of Wight. I have called the tape "Meditational Serenity" by Simon Corkery.

Young Simon was getting on very well at the De la Salle Brothers school in Skibbereen, he took a very active part in concerts and sketches which were put on in the town hall for parents friends and teachers. He did well in his studies and at weekends and on other occasions sang in the Church Choir in Clonakilty, which Sarah did also.

Eileen finished her studies in Southampton and I went over to see her get her degree as I had when Angela received hers. When Eileen finished her teacher training she was not able to get a post, so she came home and worked in a local bar until she managed to get a part-time teaching post in Midleton, where she stayed with one of the Knights whose family were very good to her.

At this time she took part in a play in Rossmore which they performed for the All Ireland Drama Festival. She had to blacken her face and stuff her dress with pillows to look like a black Mama. She was used to the accent from the coloured community she lived and worked with in Southampton. They did very well in the competition, and had to travel around to other festivals. Later she was to get a position teaching the mentally handicapped. The night Eileen left the bar to take up teaching, the staff threw a party for her, once again down in our shop, so it saw great times.

Angela and Peter had come over to Ireland for a holiday after Angela got her degree in Sculpture and Fine Art. When I went for the conferring I saw all her work and it was magnificent. She brought some of it home with her, but more had to be dismantled to make room for the work of the next set of students work. I was told to encourage Angela to go on to Trinity College in Dublin to study for her Masters degree, as Jonah-Jones from Trinity was one of the assessors to go to Norwich to assess the work. Peter liked Ireland and a few months later they came over to live in the caravan that we had. Peter was employed by Houlihans Bakery and was very well accepted and got on very well, making many friends. They brought a small cottage near Carrigfadda and stayed with us while they got it ready to live in. Angela didn't bother going to college and their first son Jonathan was born soon after they moved into the cottage and once again the shop came into use for a Christening Party. She taught art in Clonakilty Vocational School in the evenings and at a later date she taught in Ballydehob and Lisheen.

John came home one year for Christmas, the one year when the roads became impassable with frozen snow for several days. Aunt Kathleen came to us for Christmas, I think the first time she had ever been invited out for Christmas dinner with her relations. She thoroughly enjoyed it with the family. Other Christmases, her very good neighbours the Bartley's had seen that she had a nice day. They used to take in a Christmas tree and dress it for her, the children would bring her presents and they would play tapes of music for her, they were extremely good to her.

Elizabeth came home often. She worked in the bank for a year or so and then branched into the Inland Revenue and has moved up the ladder very quickly getting through all her courses. She was very keen on dancing and athletics, aerobics, water ski-ing and horse riding and many other activities and led a really busy life.

Another welcome visitor to Ballyduvane was Sr Mary Annette (Kathleen) who was Aunt Kathleen's namesake. They got on very well together and Sr Mary Annette used to spend a lot of time visiting and chatting with her Aunt, who was also very fond of Baby — Sr Mary Annette's mother and my stepmother. She kept Kathleen informed of all the family news and how everyone was doing.

Baby herself had died shortly after we came to Ireland so we travelled to

Longford in the three wheeler. The roads were strange to us and it was dark and wet before we reached Longford. There was a very large attendance at the funeral, and even the travelling people from all round Longford were there, and it showed that like her mother before her, she was always good to the less fortunate. It was a sad occasion, but she had Fr Eamonn and Sister Mary Annette with her when she died, so she was truly blessed.

Aunt Kathleen had worked hard all her life, her neighbours and friends were very fond of her, and always calling to make sure that she was all right. One day going home after visiting some friends near to her, as I passed the end of her road, I had a sudden feeling that something was wrong. I turned the car in the road and went up to Kathleen's house. As I went in the door I could hear her crying with pain, so I called the doctor and the priest, and it was decided that I should stay with her. For seven weeks I stayed with her night and day, Elsie and good neighbours relieving me at times and Con and Mary sitting with me at night time to keep me company, they had been used to calling every night to see her and did all her messages and took her to town when needed., Con was like a son to her. At last Kathleen had to be admitted to Bandon Hospital as she was getting very weak, and from there she was transferred to Clonakilty Hospital.

Aunt Kathleen had passed for teaching in her young days, but she did not take it up, she stayed with the McSweeney aunt and uncles and looked after them on the farm. She would discuss our entry into the Common Market, and she was up to date with all the world news as she listened to the radio a lot and read the newspapers. She had a great interest in everything for one so old. The television reception was not so good, but when she first had it, all the neighbours would come in to watch. Aunt Kathleen had a great philosophy of life and one could sit for hours listening to her, also she had a fantastic memory and it was great to be able to hear about the days of Lord Carbery and what it was like going to school with people like Michael Collins. She became very fond of Elsie and would sit and tell her stories about the past. After she was taken to Clonakilty Hospital, Elsie would visit her and Kathleen was very relaxed and happy there, she thought it was great to have the nuns and the priest on call. However Elsie went to visit her one afternoon, and she thought she was asleep but when she called the nurse, they found she had passed peacefully away.

Daddy, Aunt Madge, Uncle Michael, Uncle Nelius and Aunt Maud had all died while I was in England. So it was that, that generation of Corkerys had all passed away and when Fr John came down from Longford to offer up the Requiem Mass for her, he was very lonely after her, as were her neighbours and all of us and I had at least been able to be with her and help relieve her suffering at the end of her days. I shall always be grateful to her neighbours, the Bartleys for the use of their telephone, night or day, because when Kathleen was most in pain, I was able to consult with Dr Quirke who was constant in his attendance. The clergy of Rossmore and Bealad whom Kathleen held in great esteem were also very good in bringing Holy Communion to her. She appreciated this and was generous to them in the settling of her affairs, also to the Peru and African Missions, and the training of young men for the priesthood. As she said to me one day "I came into this world with nothing, and I am going out the same".

That reminds me of a Mission in Rossmore long ago when I remember the Missioner always gave the text of the sermon before making the sign of the cross and starting preaching. "What doth it profit a man if he gain the whole world and suffer the loss of his Immortal soul?" This was the thinking of Aunt Kathleen, and it has been mine during all these years. That is why I appeal to my fellow emigrants who are embarking on lifes journey — get to the top by all means because God has given you talents, and it is up to you to use them wisely and be just and charitable in all your dealings. You will find in England especially, that if you treat your fellow citizens with justice and honesty, they will be firm in their friendship and will remain loyal to you also.

There are so many ways you can make comparisons with the culture I was brought up with before emigrating and the change that has come over our country on my return. Materialism has destroyed our Irish culture, not so much in rural Ireland, but definitely in our cities.

Vatican II teachings have been slow in coming into practice in Ireland in comparison with the churches across the water. During the last ten years we have improved considerably, and under the guidance of his Lordship Bishop Michael Murphy and his assistant Bishop John Buckley we have made strides in laiety participation in the work of the parish, especially in our parish in Rosscarbery. The liturgy has now been developed in the same way as Bishop Worlock, now Archbishop of Liverpool, had done in the Portsmouth diocese, which I had benefited from. Our whole life was participation in the Church, during the periods I was not nursing. Church cleaning groups were set up, coffee mornings after Mass, where we made enough money to send handicapped children to Lourdes, Parish Councils with representatives to the Diocesan Council, issuing Mass leaflets and papers and Parish news bulletins at the church door and the Mass itself. Offertory processions, ministers of the word and ministers of the Eucharist. Our church had a strong choir and a good youth club. There was an opportunity for everyone of whatever age group to take full participation in parish affairs. The Catholic Women's League was the mainstay of the ladies participation in the Parishes, the St Vincent de Paul, the Legion of Mary, the third order of St. Francis, Catholic Guides and Scouts and other groups were all busy. The Knights, the Catenians, and the Altar servers, all had their own organisations, so there are plenty of activities that our emigrants now leaving this country can take part in across the water. The names and addresses of these organisations and telephone numbers are on the notice boards in the churches, or any member of the parish would only be too pleased to help with enquiries. "Life" support groups to help single parent families are available as well, along with the Samaritans and numerous other groups to help in any worry or trouble.

In Ireland we have our Knights in this country helping at advice centres, throughout the provinces, covering the information centres for those intending to emigrate. Together with the Bishop's representatives they are helping to man these centres. I mention this, because people say to me "What do the Knights do?" They work quietly in their parishes helping the clergy and Hierarchy wherever they are required. The Cork area has its main centre at 32 South Terrace in the city where one of the emigration advice centres is situated. Soon after joining the Knights in Ireland I became secretary of our local Council and later Grand Knight. I have already addressed a Provincial meeting in the Portsmouth diocese of how the Knights over here could, with the help of the Knights of St Columba, help our emigrants in the South of England. Many of our members are also members of St Vincent de Paul, who work so hard, in all parishes to help the needy and less fortunate in Ireland.

I was talking to Alice Taylor concerning my autobiography and she told me there was a great need for me to compare the two cultures of Ireland and England, this is why I am bringing these points to the fore as I have experienced in my dealings since returning to West Cork.

One other main difference I see, is the respect and dignity that is shown in this country to our dead, compared with the low attendance at funerals and the loneliness that is evident in the funerals in England. Three large cars to the church and then maybe on to the crematorium, seems so abrupt an event in comparison to the sympathy and generosity shown by neighbours and friends here, the crowds that gather to support the family at the home or the funeral parlour and again at the graveside. Funeral parlours are in use in England too but my experience is that only close relatives pay a visit to the deceased and then the closed coffin is brought to the house of the deceased or near relative and waits outside to be joined by the close relations in another hired car, and then off on its last journey, a few neighbours might attend or maybe workmates but that is all.

Compare a wedding over in England, and then compare it with a funeral, the people are lining the streets uninvited and waving when a pretty bride arrives at, or near the church. Total strangers will wave and express themselves, as I have experienced myself having three weddings of three of my daughters in England.

I remember Fr Donnelly our Parish Priest in Shanklin, one morning after Mass, when I joined him in his house for a cup of coffee, asking me if I would come with him to a funeral of an old Irish lady in the Island who had passed away. I was the only person except maybe one other at the graveside, and her rosary and medals were passed on to me, as there was no one else to receive them. On other occasions, you would see maybe a funeral as I described already, dash across the traffic lights and speed away to be lost in a few

Our children now grown up

Our grandchildren in England

minutes, in the main stream of traffic, with no concern of any one, just a passing glimpse of some loved one on their way to the grave — so cold and so calculated — these are my observations for what they are worth. These things maybe would not happen in a small village where the people all know each other, but elsewhere, people are always on the move and not known even by their immediate neighbours, life and death just pass everyone by.

Another of my observations is in dealing with getting work done here, such as house repairs, or improving a place. Here you will get the handshake and the promise of someone coming to do the job and maybe a year later you will be lucky, where as in England, if you want something done, you are given an estimate that evening or maybe the next day, the estimates are usually accurate and good value for money is given.

It takes a while to get used to the Irish way of life again, after being businesslike across the water for so many years. The Irish way of life is more relaxing certainly and one gradually accepts things philosophically and takes life as it comes, instead of always worrying about tomorrow, this way of life is what attracts so many tourists, because they can enjoy relaxed holidays where everyone has time for them and willing to stop and chat and be truly hospitable and probably bring them in for a cup of tea and whiskey and sherry and a cut of brown cake or buns and apple tart or sit them down for a meal.

When the Irish go to England, they seem a different kind of person, they work all the hours that God can spare them, and are a great credit to their country. The Irish nurses are terribly popular in England, I think it is their warm hearted ways that make them attractive to their patients. Irish priests are very popular as well and easily gain the confidence of their congregations. We have a gift as ambassadors of good humour and participation, I hope we never change. Whenever I return to the Isle of Wight to see my children, all the old parishoners come rushing over to me to greet me, and you can see the joy on their faces. Even on my visit to the Conservative Club in Shanklin the English come rushing over as soon as they hear me speak, they know my voice straight away. I am not saying that in a boastful way, but I am speaking of my experiences on so many occasions. On the other hand I have found out since moving back to Ireland that you could not find nicer neighbours, they are co-operative, understanding and generous to Elsie and myself and fully accept her.

The Cable Car at Lourdes

CHAPTER XXIV

Soon after Aunt Kathleen died, Elsie and I had a chance to join the Rosscarbery pilgrimage to Lourdes with Fr McGrath and Fr Bertie O'Mahony as our leaders. Apart from Rosscarbery people, there were a few from Clonakilty who we knew and also a few from Leap and other areas. A coach was to take us to the airport, but all day we had messages about delays because of some industrial action or other. Eventually it was night time before we actually went to the airport, only to be told that we would have a few hours more to wait. Nothing was going to daunt this party on their journey. John Joe Hicks brought out his accordian and soon there was quite a party going. The airport staff seemed to enjoy it too, as it was to be a long night for them before we took off around six o'clock in the morning. We arrived circling round Lourdes to find it fog bound, away then to Toulouse where we landed, waiting as we thought for a coach to take us to Lourdes. However the fog lifted, we were able to take off again and arrived at the hotel Jean d'Arc in time to get some breakfast. The journey back home too was disorganised, we had to leave Lourdes around four o'clock in the morning, but it was all well worth it — to visit Lourdes is a real experience.

Having been very tired after our travels most of us had a rest and later that evening made our way down towards the Grotto to familiarise ourselves with the surroundings. We watched from a distance the torch-light procession which usually takes place between 8 p.m. and 9 p.m. The first day after Mass at the Basilica we did the large Stations of the Cross. John L. O'Sullivan was one of our pilgrims and he was in a wheelchair, and going up the steps of the Stations we had to spoke the wheels spoke by spoke, his wheelchair kept coming back again. So I suggested I pull the chair up backwards. Michael Tobin and myself and a couple of others helped out, by the time we had finished the fourteen stations we felt we were really physically and mentally orientated pilgrims.

The time passed very quickly between itinerary times for devotion and meal times. The day we went to the baths I followed John L. and I had the pleasure of wheeling him afterwards where I was with him for the Blessing of the sick. John L. was very cold looking after he came out of the baths and I did not have to dry myself as I was dry by the time I came to put on my clothes. One morning we had Mass at an altar in the open on the left hand side of the Basilica and Fr Bertie O'Mahony was offering up the Mass and when it came to the "Consecration of the Mass" birds flew round in a circle round the altar it was a lovely sight, and I think everyone that attended that Mass will always remember that. The only time I have ever seen that since, was when Fr O'Driscoll raised his hand to bless the statue of Our Lady of Lourdes which we erected in the Mall School, the martins or swallows swept low in a complete circle round the Grotto and the thirty people present were amazed at it as well.

One afternoon the ladies were going to the baths, and most of the men decided to go up in the cable car that goes across to a hill which is almost

Lourdes

opposite the Basilica. Johnny Brown, myself and Michael Tobin were holding on to a chain behind us, and trying to look brave. Michael with his auburn hair was there standing up holding on to the chain as if he was at school, hands behind the back addressing the class, his face pale. Johnny Brown in the middle, half laughing, half shaking, and who comes up to us but Fr Bertie himself all six feet of him looking very erect, and smiling to himself. He approached the three of us and he addressed Johnny "Would you like me to hear your confession", "God knows am I not bad enough without you coming here to me about confession" or some such comical remark. This is a memory Johnny and I when we meet at stations and other social occasions, we always refer to, and Johnny always has a good laugh. We passed another cable car going in the opposite direction and as it slowed down we thought we were stuck and that we might be there all day. We were glad to come out on the hill or mountain, and we saw some St Bernard dogs on that hill. Our journey to St Bernadette's home was a lovely journey and we brought back a piece of the stone from the house where she looked after the sheep. Our last evening at the Grotto was a memorable one, a moment of quiet peace entered your mind and a feeling of loneliness came over me and Elsie felt the same, it was leaving behind a very close friend and we both told Our Lady in our thoughts that we would return, which I hope to do if God spares us. Such a wonderful pilgrimage after looking after Kathleen R.I.P. for so many weeks, and then the peace of mind that comes to you in the presence of Our Lady is hard to describe. You get that feeling at Knock, as I have paid a yearly visit to Knock with the Knights of St Columbanus every year, and privately several times since. As it says in the Penny Catechism "A lifting of the mind and heart to God".

The Knights in Ireland like their colleagues in Great Britain, undertake projects, such as taking caravans all the way to Italy to give help to the people of a flood stricken area. They have also helped the children of Northern Ireland to go on holidays away from the troubles. We had two girls come to stay with us. As you can imagine they were very nervous. One night there was a bit of a bang outside. We thought they had disappeared, but found them huddled together in one bed right beneath the bed clothes. They attended an Irish Night in the Emmet Hotel and sang for the audience who were enraptured by their performance.

It so happened that while they were with us, we received an unexpected visit from one of the Knights from the Isle of Wight who was visiting his parents at Garretstown. He asked us to take the children over to the farm, which we did. It was the highlight of their holiday. They were able to run around, collect the eggs from the hens, but what delighted them most was the big sow with her piglets, by their description, she was as big as the house itself, they were rushing in saying she was enormous. It was a happy coincidence that Paddy who had enjoyed the visit of the Northern Ireland children to the Island, met them here too.

Angela and Peter who lived near Carrigfada now had a little girl called Catherine. Jonathan their little boy suffered a lot with infantile eczema and asthma and spent many spells in the Mercy Hospital in Cork, and Angela would stay up there with him. We often went to visit them in their house, and near to them was an old disused school. It somehow attracted me every time I went past it, and a few times I stopped and looked in the windows. I then got Eileen interested in it, also Elsie and the others. Simon by this time was attending the Regional College in Galway studying Hotel Management, I found it difficult financially to pay his fees and keep the shop open as well. One day Angela told us that the school was for sale, so I thought if I could sell the shop and buy it I might be able to manage, another factor being that at this time Elsie had been in hospital with a bad back and found the shop heavy going with lifting goods. The whole family thought I was utterly and completely mad, but I went ahead and sold the shop and bought the old Mall School which had not been used as a school for eleven years and had become rather derelict looking.

It was a fine structural building, and I accepted the challenge of putting it back into circulation, because it was during this period that a lot of students and others from Western Europe were buying up all the old cottages and properties in West Cork. It was the era for getting back to country life and self sufficiency. The school in its day had been a great centre for the local community, not only as a school but as a dance hall and a polling station. Of course we could hardly hold dances, but we agreed to let it continue to be used as a polling station, and we used to look forward to elections. The polling booths would be set up in the living room, and a long table for the officials to sit at. Out in the entrance hall, which had once been the school cloakroom, people from the various political parties would gather, along with the personators, who checked the names off on the electoral roll as people arrived to cast their vote. Posters appeared all round the gates, in the centre of the crossroads outside and on the telegraph poles nearby. There was a sort of festive atmosphere all day, plenty of people to chat to, and a chance to see all the neighbours, it would seem very quiet when the last vote had been cast, the boxes removed and the booths taken down to be taken away until the next election day.

We took the caravan from Ballyduvane and in August we moved it into the schoolyard, where we stayed while the school was renovated, moving into the actual building for Christmas. It was a novelty living in the caravan. Sometimes we could hear mice scampering round inside the walls. Elsie had a fur coat, and rather than put it inside the school with the rest of our possessions which were packed away in tea chests, she kept it in the wardrobe in the caravan. One day she went to the wardrobe and as she opened the door she let out a scream and tried to pounce on a little mouse that had jumped over her shoulder, and away down the hole under one of the seats which became beds at night time. When she looked at her coat, the shoulder had been nibbled away, and a nest made in the pocket, luckily the nest was empty still.

We were now in Rosscarbery parish, but I went to daily Mass in Leap as it was the nearest for the post, shopping etc. I joined the Legion of Mary in Leap

The Mall School when we moved there

Dail Election

CONSTITUENCY OF CORK SOUTH-WEST

Polling Station No. 44

Simon Corkery's House, Cloonkeen

Polling District - **23** SR

parish as there was no presidium in Rosscarbery and I became very active within the organisation, and I still continued my weekly visits to Clonakilty Hospital where every Monday I spent two or three hours talking to the patients in the large sitting room and providing them with Catholic books, magazines and papers and Readers Digests, and I went round the male wards as well.

I had a great send off from the Legion of Mary branch in Clonakilty where I had spent some happy years. The president Miss Sheeley presented me with a framed photograph of Pope John Paul II at a lovely meal provided by them in Fernhill Hotel and of course Elsie was invited too. I became very friendly with Fr Burke in Leap, and of course with my Parish Priest Fr McGrath and Fr White and became secretary of Leap Legion of Mary. We were a very active branch and a lot of house visits of the sick were done by the female members. There were pilgrimages to Knock annually, and the acies where the local groups all meet together.

The most exciting visit to Knock we ever had was in September 1979 when the Pope came to Ireland. This was when we first moved up to the school and were living in the caravan. Elsie came with me, also Sarah who had now been confirmed by Bishop Lucey in Clonakilty and finished National School and was now attending secondary school, but still in Clonakilty.

We set off very early in the morning to catch the special train from Cork which would take us to Claremorris, and thence by coach to Knock. We all arrived on a damp misty day, clad in raincoats, hats and the place was a sea of coloured umbrellas. It was a day that no one will ever forget, the first sight of the helicopter with the Pope aboard as it came in to land beside the Basilica. The wonderful Mass and talk given by the Holy Father, his journey through the vast crowds in his Popemobile, and then the sad hush as he left us again going up into the darkening sky and away from us again. No one wanted to see him go. The crowds were fantastic during the long wait, so good humoured despite the bad weather sharing their sandwiches and flasks, everyone united in one cause to see and hear the Pope. Something that had never happened in Ireland before. The long day over, the journey home was not quite so easy. Buses had been provided to convey the people back to Claremorris, but it was dark and raining and people were pushing to get on the buses. I managed to get on a bus, but Elsie and Sarah who were right beside me were bodily pushed to the back of the crowd — they could not get on the bus, and I could not get off, and we got separated. They had to walk the six or seven miles to Claremorris, but before they got half way, the bus drivers had refused to move because they couldn't run the risk of knocking people down in the crowds who were walking right across the road in front of the buses. There was no alternative route, so it was just chaos. We found each other again and eventually reached Claremorris railway station, surprised and delighted to see the train still waiting there, which in fact it did for another hour or two until every passenger had been accounted for.

Knock Shrine

We have now been living in the school for ten years, the three wheeler car that we brought with us has long since gone, and we have progressed to having a proper four wheeled car. We have made several trips to Longford and back to England and the Isle of Wight.

After Angela, Simon was the next to marry; while he was in Galway Regional he met a lovely girl, they married here but returned to the Isle of Wight where they are rearing five gorgeous children. Eileen was the next to marry, she also married here, and is still living here with her Irish husband Pat and has three lovely children. She still teaches the mentally handicapped children. Angela and Peter had another son just after they moved from Carrigfada to Clonakilty to be near Peter's work and they have since returned to the Isle of Wight. John got married in England to Ann and now has two sons, and Elizabeth also got married in England to Phil and has a son and daughter. Now this last year our youngest daughter Sarah who went nursing to the Isle of Wight got married to Carey, so we are alone again.

What with weddings, christenings, first communions and conferrings, like when John got his B.A. this year, there is plenty of travelling to do, back and forth across the Irish Sea. I suppose with five children and twelve grandchildren across the water, there will be plenty more travelling to come. We brought the children home, hoping for a better way of life for them, but gradually they have gone back to the Isle of Wight one by one.

I have worked closely with four different priests, and each and everyone of them have been pleasant, grateful and understanding. Each has left his own legacy of holiness in the parish. I have enjoyed it immensely here, a lot has been achieved — a new hall to be proud of and the community spirit which abounded while that was going on, and the draws, the raffles, the meetings here in the school while the hall was being built, the ladies meetings here on Monday nights, the laughter and the crack, and the pleasure we got from these meetings was worth every effort that was put into it. The bed push from Clonakilty to Skibbereen organised by the youth club towards the hall funds, the support from our friends in Rosscarbery, the pub talent competitions culminating in a cabaret in the hall, the drama group evenings, the dances at Christmas time, the Feis and exhibition of Irish dancing that still goes on at the hall, the school concerts — the talents of the people of Carrigfada are too numerous to mention, and to put into this book.

I had several bouts of illness during these years and many a night I lay awake with burning pains in my stomach, until Dr Murray sent me to Dr Whelton at the Regional Hospital, and under his guidance and, later under Dr Joan Power who was a charming person and took a personal interest in my history and treatment. To Dr Barrett, Dr Quirke and Dr Murray, to Dr Curtin I owe a great deal. After four or five years, things were improving until four years ago, the gullet was going into spasm. Dr O'Brien came to see me one Sunday morning when he was acting as locum, and having consulted with Dr Murray I had an appointment to see the consultant surgeon Mr G. O'Sullivan from near

The School as it is now

The School and the Grotto

Skibbereen who saw me at the Mercy Hospital in Cork. He had me admitted into hospital and together with Dr Bennett, when they took me to the theatre on the Friday for investigations, they were able to find the cause of my distress. The following Tuesday Mr O'Sullivan operated on me, major surgery to repair my hiatus hernia, and under his skills the operation was a great success. I was in intensive care for about twelve hours, and then made a marvellous recovery thank God. The only sad part was the depression that set in about a week after coming home. I lost all my confidence and Elsie God help her, had a trying time with me for about six months. My mind was in a turmoil but thanks to Fr David McAuliffe and my very good friends in Myross Wood and the prayers of the people of the parish, I had a complete recovery.

I have still to go to hospital at different times for dilation of the oesophagus — my thanks go out to the nuns and sisters and nursing staff of St Patrick's ward in the Mercy Hospital for all their kind attention during these last four years. I have to mention Dr. Breden the chest specialist at the Regional Hospital who has been very good to me also, and kept me under his care during these years.

It is in gratitude to Our Lady for all the favours I have received from her over the years and continue to do so, that I got a statue of Our Lady of Lourdes erected in the grounds of the Mall School, not only because I was grateful to her in that way, but it was the Marian Year, and I thought this could be my contribution in this Holy Year, so that devotion to Our Lady would spread, as it already has begun in this area. I must thank Con and Marie for their great kindness to me during Elsie's visits to England and for allowing me to put the grotto in the gateway between their house and ours. I am grateful to the Murphy's for the gravel they provided and of course to Sean Collins who erected the grotto and the clergy who blessed the grotto and the kind words and compliments paid to Elsie and myself on that occasion. It was an occasion in which some of the past pupils of the school were able to participate, including of course Con and Sean. Also some of the sisters from Glandore who we knew on the Isle of Wight came along too. The school means so much to the people of the area, that I hope those of you, who know me now, will remember me when I have gone across the "Great Divide" that awaits each and everyone of us.

I must thank Fr McGrath for choosing me to assist the clergy in giving out Holy Communion in the parish. In all humility I feel as I did then, unworthy of such a great privilege. It has been a joy for me to help in any way I could because without the guidance of our priests, where would we be? We are very privileged to have three priests in our family, Fr. John, Fr Eamonn and now my nephew Fr Noel McGeeney who is working in Nigeria.

To all the neighbours, the Hill families, the O'Mahony's, the McCarthy families, above and below me, to all the parishioners of Carrigfadda, and I mean one and all, my thanks for allowing me into your hearts and minds, to all the members of the Reenascreena Community Council I say "keep up the good work!". To the neighbours who invited me there on the occasions of their

Neighbours and friends at the Blessing of the grotto May 13th 1988

Photo of three priests concelebrating Mass at Fr. Noel McGeeney's First Mass in Longford Cathedral nephew of two priests.

weddings, a big thank you. There is one personality in the parish of Carrigfadda whose smile, and hearty laughter, has brought joy, not only to all the clergy over the years, as Sacristan, but to all who have enjoyed her hard work in the Ladies Club, and elsewhere and to whose wedding her mother, invited Elsie and myself, namely Joan O'Mahony whom we now know as Mrs Cottrill. To Joan and Ben my greatest gratitude.

I saw Joan the morning of her wedding, sweeping out the sacristy in her working clothes, and then a couple of hours later, walking up the aisle with a beautiful radiant smile on her face. I go as far as to say, that down at Ownahincha with Ben in the sunlight overlooking the sea, no princess could ever look so happy. "God bless you both always."

The other work I was involved in was the Rosary Crusade which I took part in during the abortion referendum. Having approached Fr McGrath he suggested I should seek permission from Monsignor Michael Daly P.P. V.G., he was chaplain to the Knights in that area it was easy to approach him. I submitted a notice in writing addressed to all parish priests in the area, to have a Rosary Crusade commencing on August 15th in Timoleague to ask Our Lady of Knock to enlighten the minds and hearts of the Irish people to giving a satisfactory result at the polling booths of the right of life to the unborn child. I went to see each priest in turn and everywhere I went I was received with courtesy and the willingness of their cooperation in making the Rosary Crusade a success. Masses were offered as well as the recitation of the Rosary at a time convenient to the needs of the parishioners. We had a concelebrated Mass at Timoleague beside Our Lady's Grotto, followed by the Rosary where pilgrims came every year to do the rounds and drink water from the well there: following in to Barryroe, Clonakilty, Rossmore, Bealad, Rosscarbery, Leap, Glandore, Union Hall, Castletownsend, Skibbereen, Lisheen and finishing up near to a church on the road to Ballydehob. It was very well supported by all, and this was supported by all organisations in the different parishes. The concluding prayers were recited during a reconciliation service of readings and prayers alternated by hymns, where all organisations within the parish of Clonakilty took part. I attended all the evening recitations of the rosary and the weather on the whole was favourable. Other Knights took part in the distribution of leaflets. Family Solidarity and other speakers made public addresses and were eagerly listened to. It was sad to see criticism of the clergy who spoke out in the defence of the unborn child; after all they were only doing what they were ordained to do "Go out to the whole world and proclaim the good news". We had the support of other churches as well, and after all, the people of Ireland were only exercising their democratic vote. The Referendum on Divorce which followed on after this, was again the right of the Irish people to vote for the principles which so many of our forefathers gave their lives for. As I have already said in this book, we have to live according to the Christian teachings of our church and school and bring up our children in these traditions. We have a country with a constitution guaranteeing the right of all denominations the freedom to express themselves, and we thank God that we have won that freedom, when you look at Eastern block countries who have no freedom such as we have here. Then we must live in harmony with our neighbours in peace, justice and living the Christian way of life, by giving witness to Christ in our own lives, by the way we act and to speak with charity about all peoples. We must not throw away our culture and our inheritance for some meaningless and materialistic way of life, we must not take our example from the soap operas on television or the headlines of the media; if we do that we must be living in cuckoo land. If we follow the lives of the great stars of Hollywood, we will see that all the oscars in the world and all the wealth that goes with it, they have not found the happiness that they expected. Some of these stars have managed to be exemplary in the practice of their faith, and kept a balance between what is good and what is evil. Without respect for the Creator, who created us, and to whom we owe everything in Life, we cannot accept the problems of life, and it is from the strength we get from Him, that we keep our sense of balance, in love for our neighbour and preparing ourselves for the journey beyond. In our parishes you will see ordinary people who have faced terrninal illnesses with candour and resignation, with a smile coming through in the midst of pain, that would touch the hearts and minds of all Christians. I have experienced this on so many occasions during the last three years — those whose lives have touched holy priests and nuns who have said it openly. If my health had been better about five years ago I attended a seminar on two occasions in Dublin to join in the Viatore Christi, where Catholics and other Christian bodies work together in the third world. Elsie and myself were prepared to live out our lives in Sudan or where we were wanted. Even now I feel like doing it to give services to others who are less fortunate. Bishop Lucey R.I.P. who worked so hard during his years as Bishop of Cork and Ross gave up his remaining years in going out to hot climates to serve these people. Surely if such an eminent member of the church could set that example to us in his year of retirement, it should bring home to us the humility with which he was endowed and would not Ireland be a better place instead of bickering about the liberalisms we so much seek, and be content with our lot in life and be thankful to God for what we have got. Then Charlie would not have to rely on Fiscal Rectitude and Garrett on Economics and we would not be so much inward looking in our thinking; but outward looking as indeed most Irish people are, we would be a better nation on the whole. As these are my concluding remarks to close fifty years of memories of my travels during war and peace, I have tried to be myself throughout, I have not followed certain guide lines as to how an Autobiography should be written. I want the reader to come with me in spirit as it were, to look behind that smiling mask, which my thoughts portray in this book. I hope I have given my readers pleasant reading and maybe food for thought in their own lives and if you recognised value for thought towards those around you, then this book will have brought to the fore a character that is light hearted, warms to feelings, and if it pleases you, pass it on to a friend. I hope your criticisms will be just, and fair, and if I have hurt anyone in my memories of travel I apologise in advance. God bless you all, to those who agree and to those who disagree. Go neirí an bothar libh go léir.

A Tribute To The Knights

(Extracts from local Isle of Wight Press)

NOVEMBER 27th 1971

Protecting The Decent Way Of Life

Among those at the dinner were Bro. Peter Hatcher (Provincial Grand Knight), Bro. Simon Corkery (Grand Knight), Bro. Michael May (Supreme Knight). Councillor John Groome (Deputy Mayor of Ryde) and Councillor Patrick Bryan (Mayor of Newport and a past Grand Knight).

1972

KNIGHTS OF ST. COLUMBA GIVE HOLIDAY

ISLAND OPENS DOORS TO BELFAST CHILDREN

Three-hundred-and-sixty children are being given a break from the horror of strife-torn Belfast by the Knights of St Columba, a Roman Catholic organization, which is bringing them to England for a ten-day holiday.

"The children are from Protestant and Catholic families," explained Mr. Simon Corkery, of Atherley Road, Shanklin, the Isle of Wight Grand Knight, today.

They will be divided into groups and shared between Knights of St Columba regions throughout England and Wales.

Ten of the children will be staying with families in the Portsmouth region which includes the Island. And four of these will be holidaying in the Sandown-Shanklin district .... two at Shanklin, two at Lake.

The children arrive tomorrow to begin their holidays.

"Next Sunday we are bringing all the Portsmouth area children together for a round-the-island tour and we hope to give them a day out they will always remember," said Mr. Corkery.

Yesterday the Church of the Sacred Heart, Shanklin, Youth Club gave a donation and the Knights of St Columba ran a fundraising stall outside the Sacred Heart following masses.

After the Island tour, nuns at St Anthony's convent, Shanklin, will be running a party at the convent for the children.

"If any groups or people would like to help the holiday fund with donations we should be most grateful," said Mr. Corkery.

APRIL 25th 1974

KNIGHTS CELEBRATE SILVER JUBILEE

It was a time for memories at Ryde on Friday when the Isle of Wight Council of the Knights of St. Columba celebrated their silver jubilee at a dinner dance at The Oasis.

The company of more than 160 included Knights from Portsmouth, Southampton, Bournemouth, Winchester, Eastleigh and Gosport, and the principal guests were the Roman Catholic Bishop of Portsmouth, the Right Rev. Derek Worlock and Supreme Knight, Mr. Martin Cairns.

The Grand Knight, Mr. H. Lloyd Bunce of Lake, said seven of the 57 brothers who were initiated at the formation of the council in 1949, were still members and several of them were present that evening.

Recalling the early days of the Council, he referred to the late Father Michael O'Riordan, who was parish priest at Shanklin and the late Captain Herbert Ward.

"For many years, Father O'Riordan was Chaplain of the Council and despite ill-health was a man of great activity and enthusiasm. No one who ever met Father O'Riordan could ever forget him. He left a fragrant memory," said Mr. Lloyd Bunce.

Of Captain Ward, the grandson of William George Ward, a strong Tractarian and contemporary of John Henry Newman, Mr. Lloyd Bunce said: "He was our first Grand Knight and saw the Council through a very difficult period and it was largely through his effort that the Council survived."

Mr. Lloyd Bunce, who was proposing the toast "The Hierarchy, clergy and guests," said it was the first time the council had welcomed the Bishop at one of their functions and they were conscious of the honour.

The Bishop, proposing the toast to the Order of the Knights of St. Columba, spoke of the welcome changes that had taken place in attitudes over the past 25 years, and the growing oneness of the clergy, people and organisations.

Outward Looking Policy

The outward-looking policy of the Order in the service of the community, was referred to by Mr. Maurice Cairns, who spoke of the special committees started by the Knights and comprising people regardless of religion and creed, to rally public opinion on vital community issues and direct the concensus of that opinion at the most effective target ... their local Members of Parliament.

He said more than 140 such committees had been formed throughout England and Wales and it was hoped to start similar committees in Scotland.

The seven brothers initiated in 1949 and who qualified for jubilee awards were Brothers McGarity, Little, Hogan, Johnson, Gallagher, Flux and Lloyd Bunce.

Mr. S. Corkery of Shanklin, a Past Knight of the Isle of Wight Council, announced arrangements were being made so that Island Catholics and others could support the anti-abortion rally at Hyde Park, London.

Arrangements for the dinner dance were made by Mr. D. Sullivan, of Shanklin, the Council secretary and Mr. Bill Russell, the social secretary.

Before the celebration dinner, the Knights and their guests attended a Concelebrated Mass at St. Mary's Church, Ryde, at which the Bishop presided.

OCTOBER 31st 1975

FROM ISLAND TO IRELAND

There will be the traditional Irish greeting of "A Hundred Thousand Welcomes" for touring Islanders who drop in at the general store at Ballyduvane, just a shillelagh throw from Clonakilty in County Cork.

As from next week, behind the counter, full of blarney and good cheer, will be Mr. Simon Corkery of Atherley Road, Shanklin. Or maybe his wife, Elsie.

The Corkerys and two of the younger members of their family of six children. Simon (15) and Sarah (9), are leaving the Island today for their new home and business venture in Eire.

Said Mr. Corkery, born in County Longford: "It's a real wrench leaving the Island. We've made a lot of friends in 17 years."

Mr. Corkery (58), who retired for health reasons earlier this year, was Senior Enrolled Nurse at St. Mary's Hospital, Newport, and is well known throughout the Island for his outstanding contributions to welfare and community work as a member of the Roman Catholic Organisation, the Knights of St. Columba. He has twice been the Grand Knight in the Island and until his planned move to Eire was district deputy for Portsmouth, Gosport and the Isle of Wight.

As a Knight he was instrumental in bringing a party of Protestant and Catholic children to the Island for holidays from strife-torn Ulster and has been prominent in the "War on Want" scheme in conjunction with the Ryde Rotary Club. He also led groups of Islanders in anti-abortion rallies in London.

Mr. Corkery, who came over from Eire to start a nursing career in England in 1938, was an RAF Medico during the war. Mrs. Corkery has been organist at the Church of the Sacred Heart, Shanklin.

In the past few days the family have been doing a round of farewells. The Knights presented Mr. Corkery with a tountain pen and, following Mass on Sunday, the parish priest at the Sacret Heart, Father Henry Donnelly, presented the family with a clock.

Said Mr. Corkery last night: "We have got a bit of land with the shop in Ballyduvane and hope to have holiday caravans."

An Afterthought

I wrote these lines in a moment of frustration, during my RAF course in the Morse class in Blackpool.

Life is interesting, life is sweet,
Life is harmonious when we meet.
Life is weary, life is sad,
It drives me scatty, it makes me bad.
Depression and sorrow for me have no restrain,
But to continue to rack my tired brain.
A weary heart, a tired frame,
Is the result of morse, from whence it came.

Elsie the evening of our first date at the Hospital Ball

As we are now with two of our grandchildren here in Ireland

Acknowledgements

I wish to express my sincere thanks to the following people who helped me with the preparation of this book.

— *to Mary T. Ronan, Leap, who typed the original manuscript and Mary Ross, Skibbereen, who helped with the typesetting.*

— *It was my great pleasure to have the assistance of Nora Walsh in the printing of this book as she was a former pupil of my late Uncle Michael Corkery N.T. Headmaster of Rossmore N.S. I wish her continued success in her business in the future.*

— *to Mr Jim O'Keeffe, Assistant Manager A.I.B. Clonakilty who so kindly wrote the Foreword to my book and to the Manager, Mr Dan Harte for his support and assistance at all times.*

— *to the members of Reenascreena Community Council, who so kindly organised events leading up to the publication of this book.*

Finally I wish to thank very specially my wife Elsie for her kindness, patience and understanding shown to me at all times, during the countless hours which we spent together working on this book.